W9-ARE-909

Always Leading, Forever Valiant

ALWAYS LEADING
FOREVER VALIANT

Stories of the University of Michigan

1817–2017

Edited by Kim Clarke

University of Michigan Press

Ann Arbor

Copyright © 2017 by the University of Michigan
All rights reserved

This book may not be reproduced, in whole or in part, including illustrations, in any form (beyond that copying permitted by Sections 107 and 108 of the U.S. Copyright Law and except by reviewers for the public press), without written permission from the publisher.

Published in the United States of America by the
University of Michigan Press
Manufactured in China
⊗ Printed on acid-free paper

2020   2019   2018   2017   4   3   2   1

A CIP catalog record for this book is available from the British Library.

ISBN: 978-0-472-03680-6 (paper)

Generous support for this publication was provided by the University of Michigan Bicentennial Office. Please visit the official Bicentennial website (bicentennial. umich.edu), Bentley Historical Library (bentley.umich.edu), and Heritage Project (heritage.umich.edu) for additional information, resources, and events connected to the history of the University of Michigan.

Frontispiece: Burton Memorial Tower, ca. 1968. Image: Bentley Historical Library, University of Michigan Photographs Vertical File.

CONTENTS

FOREWORD

Since 1817, the University of Michigan has existed to better society. Through the decades, all of the University's work—exceptional education and research, life-changing health care, arts promotion and economic development—demonstrates our public nature and our connectedness to the world.

A confluence of people and ideas are responsible for this phenomenon.

A quirky lawyer who shared ideas with none other than Thomas Jefferson, a French Catholic priest committed to Detroit, a Presbyterian minister and abolitionist, and native peoples eager to see their children educated—all deserve our gratitude for creating what was first called the University of Michigania, and what today is recognized as one of the leading academic institutions in the world.

The University of Michigan holds a special place in American higher education, and our bicentennial affords us the opportunity to celebrate our collective achievements while also examining the complex challenges facing today's academy. For 200 years, the people of this university have debated, explored and—most significantly—shared the complexities of science, the majesty of language, the power of the arts, and the salve of medicine.

My 13 predecessors led this university with a keen eye on society's challenges and our obligations as a civic institution, and their collective leadership has helped to define and elevate our standing as a truly public university. Regardless of the era, the Michigan community has been determined to achieve the egalitarian purpose best described by President James B. Angell. "Good learning," he wrote, "is always catholic and generous. It greets all comers whose intellectual gifts entitle them to admission to the goodly fellowship of cultivated minds. It is essentially democratic in the best sense of that term."

Ours is a remarkable but imperfect world. Racial unrest, environmental threats, religious intolerance, and economic inequities all demand the academy's attention. For two centuries, Michigan students and scholars have wrestled with these issues, at times successfully and at times in ways that, through the lens of time, cause discomfort and regret. History tells us we can, and will, learn from these lapses.

No one book can capture the story of Michigan; the chapters are too numerous and the effects of our teaching, research and service are, often, beyond quantifying. And that is the beauty of higher learning and the University of Michigan: We are a place of endless, captivating stories.

Here in 2017, we will use these many episodes to position U-M for the next 100 years. Our ambition is to become the model public research university. And our mission always will be to improve the world through research and education—to build a better place for our children and grandchildren. As our stories show, there is no more noble and essential work.

Mark S. Schlissel
President
University of Michigan

ROOTS

"It is worth the effort to read the inscription to feel the inspiration it provided to the leadership of the Michigan Territory who believed so firmly and at a time so long ago that a public university was necessary for the kind of society they hoped to build. It still is."

MYSTERY ABOVE THE PILLARS

By Terrence J. McDonald

When I was dean of the College of Literature, Science, and the Arts, I had a dream. In it at some point in their busy lives, every University student, staff and faculty member would walk down State Street to view the great quotation on the pediment of Angell Hall. Reflecting on its origins, and inspired by its sentiments, they would then proceed up the steps of Angell Hall and into the astonishing intellectual world of the University of Michigan.

But then I woke up. In my travels through the University, I learned that almost no one knew there was an inscription on the pediment, and those who had noticed one often had no idea what it said or what its source was.

The inscription is a passage from the Ordinance of 1787, commonly known as the Northwest Ordinance, drafted originally by Thomas Jefferson and passed by the Continental Congress in that year. The Ordinance organized the Northwest Territory—that great stretch of land "northwest" of the original 13 American colonies—that would become the states of Michigan, Ohio, Illinois, Indiana and Wisconsin.

The inscription says: *Religion, morality, and knowledge, being necessary to good government and the happiness of mankind, schools and the means of education shall forever be encouraged.* Along with the sentiment came grants of land to be sold to fund the "means of education," thus making real the first promise of free, universal public education in the history of the world. And in 1804, Congress declared, based on this previous ordinance, that one township

Angell Hall. Image:
Eric Bronson,
Michigan Photography

3

of land (23,040 acres) in each of the Northwest states would be sold to support higher education. To this, the American Indian tribes of Michigan added 1,920 acres in the Treaty of Fort Meigs in 1817.

This passage from the Northwest Ordinance was, therefore, the birth certificate of the University of Michigan. In 1887, the famous inscription was installed in the auditorium of University Hall, the headquarters of what was then called the Literary College, later the College of Literature, Science, and the Arts. The auditorium was the celebratory heart of the University, the place where all large gatherings and meetings were held as well as lectures, dramatic and musical presentations. For years, the ordinance was what all students and all visitors saw every time they entered the auditorium.

In 1925, University Hall was condemned and scheduled for demolition; four years earlier, the Board of Regents authorized a new "Literary Building." This would become James B. Angell Hall.

When the first designs for Angell Hall were prepared in 1923, they showed the building much as it is now, with the famous phrase beautifully inscribed where it is today. However, to save money, the regents asked the building's famed architect, Albert Kahn, to build Angell Hall directly to the west of University Hall, leaving the latter open for use (which continued, amazingly, through World War II). This compromised the sight lines for the inscription from State Street. Both that decision and the inevitable effect of time on the letters make for hard reading today. It is only in the right light and with a craned neck that one can make it out.

But it is worth the effort to read the inscription to feel the inspiration it provided to the leadership of the Michigan Territory who believed so firmly and at a time so long ago that a public university was necessary for the kind of society they hoped to build. It still is.

THIS IS MICHIGAN

FOUNDERS

John Monteith

Gabriel Richard

Augustus Woodward

PRESIDENTS

1. Henry Philip Tappan (1852–1863)
2. Erastus O. Haven (1863–1869
   Henry Simmons Frieze, acting president
   (1869–1871; 1880–1882, 1887)
3. James Burrill Angell (1871–1909)
4. Harry Burns Hutchins (1909–1920)
5. Marion Leroy Burton (1920–1925)
   Alfred Henry Lloyd, acting president
   (February–September 1925)
6. Clarence C. Little (1925–1929)
7. Alexander Grant Ruthven (1929–1951)
8. Harlan Henthorne Hatcher (1951–1967)
9. Robben Wright Fleming (1968–1979)
   Allan Frederick Smith, interim president (1979)
10. Harold Tafler Shapiro (1980–1987)
    Robben Wright Fleming, interim president (1988)
11. James Johnson Duderstadt (1988–1996)
    Homer A. Neal, interim president (1996)
12. Lee Carroll Bollinger (1996–2001)
    B. Joseph White, interim president (2002)
13. Mary Sue Coleman (2002–2014)
14. Mark S. Schlissel (2014–   )

Images from top: Harry Burns Hutchins Papers, Bentley Historical Library; Alexander G. Ruthven Papers, Bentley Historical Library; President (University of Michigan) records, Bentley Historical Library; Scott Soderberg, Michigan Photography

Harry Burns Hutchins

Alexander Grant Ruthven

Harold Tafler Shapiro

Mary Sue Coleman

"To Woodward a university was a place for the conservation and the advancement of all human knowledge."

AUGUSTUS WOODWARD
A Quirky Visionary

By James Tobin

In September 1817, a little crowd gathered to dedicate a raw frame building at the corner of Congress and Bates in the village of Detroit, about a block north of where city hall now stands. Two stories high, 40 feet long by 20 feet wide, this was the first edifice that one might call the University of Michigan.

Except it wasn't called that. Not by a long shot.

The new institution—thanks to its chief designer, Augustus Brevoort Woodward, chief justice of the Supreme Court of the Michigan Territory—was supposed to be known by the tongue-twisting title of *Catholepistemiad* (pronounced *cath-oh-lep-iss-TEEM-ee-add*), a term that Woodward had dreamed up himself. He said Catholepistemiad meant "system of universal science." As a bow to the obvious, he conceded that it might also be called "the University of Michigania." His fellow Detroiters—a tough crowd of a couple thousand hunters, shopkeepers, boatmen, soldiers and half-Americanized Frenchmen—apparently just rolled their eyes. And Woodward's unpronounceable coinage helped to smother the little educational experiment before it got out of its crib.

Woodward, born in 1774 and brought up in New York City, where he graduated from Columbia College, had always been fascinated by science. As a boy he had wondered what the sun was

Augustus B. Woodward photograph collection, Bentley Historical Library

Opposite page: Map of the city of Detroit in 1835, showing the University of Michigan's original location at the intersection of Congress and Bates. Two years later the University was relocated to Ann Arbor. Image: Library of Congress, Geography and Map Division

7

1825

The Catholepistemiad—U-M's first building—on Bates Street in Detroit. Image: University of Michigan Photographs Vertical File, Bentley Historical Library

made of and soon wrote a treatise on the subject. (He theorized the existence of a sunny substance he called "electron," no relation to the subatomic particle discovered much later.)

He grew into a gangly, long-nosed, eccentric bachelor, a dead ringer for the Disney image of Washington Irving's Ichabod Crane, the ghost-ridden schoolmaster of "The Legend of Sleepy Hollow." It's even been suggested that Irving knew Woodward as a young man in New York and used his physique as a model for Ichabod. Woodward might have become such a schoolmaster had it not been for a sojourn in Washington, D.C., where he impressed a very important figure, Thomas Jefferson. As president, Jefferson wanted young men loyal to him and his Democratic-Republican Party in key positions out on the frontier. So he sent Woodward to Detroit as the Michigan Territory's chief justice, a grand title for a jack-of-all-trades political job that included drawing up new laws.

Woodward got to Detroit in 1805 just after a fire destroyed most of the village. He had been impressed by Pierre L'Enfant's elegant plan for the streets of Washington. Now he sketched a similar plan for Detroit, the remnants of which are visible in the city's six great spoke-like avenues—Jefferson (named for Woodward's hero), Gratiot, Grand River, Michigan, Fort and—that's right—Woodward Avenue. The judge, apparently with a wink, insisted he had not named the street after himself. "It runs wood-ward," he said, long before the rise of Oakland County's sprawling suburbs. "Toward the woods."

Detroiters quickly decided the judge was one odd duck, if decidedly bright. Though never married, he enjoyed the company of ladies, a number of whom he once invited to his home for a meal at which he served each guest one raisin, one almond, a tiny piece of candy and a tiny cake. His speculations in land prompted accusations of "private and sinister schemes," and though he escaped serious scandal, he was unpopular for years. In the War of 1812 he stood up to the British occupiers of Detroit. That restored his political reputation, but he still had few friends.

"He was the most interested in purely intellectual pursuits of any man at that time in Michigan," one historian wrote, "and found few to sympathize or appreciate him or his endeavors."

Reading alone night after night, Woodward brooded on the mass of new information that was crowding the world's libraries. It had to be organized, he believed, writing Jefferson in 1813: "The arrangement and classification of all human knowledge is essentially associated with its future advance and improvement."

Then, remarkably, he decided to take on the job himself. He studied every system for the classification of knowledge devised so far, from the ancient Greeks and Romans to the Chinese, the Arabs, the Hindus and Enlightenment Europeans. He convinced himself that the key to a good system would be a totally new nomenclature—a precise system of names for scholarly subjects and sciences that speakers of every language could share.

chemistry, you are of course fully aware of.

To do that for all human knowledge which was then done for one subject of it in particular might concisely designate the object contemplated.

The essential improvements then imparted to a particular science consist in the exact arrangement and classification, and the correct nomenclature.

To effect the same object in every science would require the concurrent exertion of all the men of learning of a nation, and of different nations; but the principles of a clear and distinct arrangement and classification of human knowledge, generally, must, from necessity, and in the nature of things, derive their origin from a single mind.

My attention was first devoted to this subject in the year 1788. At that time I was entirely unacquainted with what had been effected in France, in relation to the science of chemistry. My mind was however fully occupied with the other grand example of arrangement and classification, which

35384

He proceeded to divide up all knowledge and give his own names—derived, he said, from Greek—to each of 63 branches: *chymia* for chemistry, *anthropoglossica* for literature, *iatrica* for medicine, and so on.

Published in 1816 as "A System of Universal Science," this was the template Woodward applied when Detroit's leaders decided it was time to set up a system of schools for the territory. As with his city plan, Woodward sketched a grand design. He imagined a great university at the center of a spoke-like system of primary and secondary schools—a Catholepistemiad comprising 13 *didaxiim* (departments), each led by a *didactor* (professor). Where colleges on the Atlantic seaboard were wholly private, this was understood to be a public institution, supported by public funds and designed for the good of all.

On the one hand, it was a carefully drawn design with a strong foundation in the educational system of Napoleonic France, then the most innovative social force in the Western world. On the other hand, it was the kind of thing that a bookish loner in a small town dreams up when he has a lot of spare time and not much work to do.

There was no money to fund anything close to Woodward's plan, just a grade school and an "academy"—what we would call a high school. His nomenclature was officially dropped after a few years, and the school, which struggled along for a few more years, was often called simply the College of Detroit. Yet that building on Congress and Bates was, in fact, the first University of Michigan.

When Michigan became a state in 1837, the new constitution declared a do-over and re-created the university in Ann Arbor, where the departments were given their familiar names. The old experiment in Detroit was nearly forgotten. In the 1840s, when the former territorial governor Lewis Cass was a U.S. senator, someone asked him what the term "College of Detroit" had once referred to. Cass thought for a minute, then said: "Ah, I have it. The College of Detroit was the nest egg of the University of Michigan. The university had been incorporated by an act of the governor and judges, drawn up by Judge Woodward, by such a pedantic and uncouth name, that even if we could recollect it, which was difficult, we always refused to adopt, and we chose to call it the 'College of Detroit.' The name given in the act I have forgotten. Let me reflect a moment. Ah, it was the Catho—Catholepistemiad."

"He was the most interested in purely intellectual pursuits of any man at that time in Michigan," one historian wrote, "and found few to sympathize or appreciate him or his endeavors."

Opposite page: In a 10-page letter to President Thomas Jefferson in 1813, Augustus Woodward shared his concept of how to organize knowledge. Image: Library of Congress, Manuscript Division

Woodward's table of professorships in the scholastic system he envisioned. Image: University of Michigan Photographs Vertical File, Bentley Historical Library

To many of his neighbors in that isolated town on the western frontier, Woodward was little more than a tolerated kook. But we can see now that, despite his quirks, he was something of a visionary. As an early chronicler of his life wrote, "To Woodward a university was a place for the conservation and the advancement of all human knowledge." That's precisely how we define the aim of the University of Michigan today.

THIS IS MICHIGAN

VISIONARY DONORS. Forward thinking has been critical to the University's growth and impact from its first days, when American Indian tribes, in an 1817 treaty with the federal government, granted land for the "college at Detroit." Philanthropists have provided gifts of property, artwork, scientific specimens, books and cash to further the work of students and faculty. Some of the most notable campus landmarks – the Law Quad, the bronze block M, Hill Auditorium and the Diag itself – were gifts to the University. Michigan fundraising campaigns consistently set records for philanthropy in public higher education.

The Potawatomi chief Metea, one of the Native Americans who signed the 1817 Treaty of Fort Meigs, which granted land to the fledgling University of Michigania.

"No one knew where the free pursuit of knowledge would lead. That was the adventure of it."

"*A CREATION OF MY OWN*"

By James Tobin

President Henry Philip Tappan. Image: George E. Perine engraving, George E. Perine visual collection, Bentley Historical Library

It was 1852. The University of Michigan needed a leader, a true president, or it might fall apart for good.

This was its second chance and probably its last. The first try had fizzled out in Detroit years ago, when Michigan was just a backwoods territory. When Michigan joined the Union as a state in 1837, it was decided to try again, this time in Ann Arbor. But so far this was a university in name only—a few bare buildings on 40 acres of farmland, no one in charge, professors fighting, students rebelling. Someone had to put the place in shape.

A man in New York was recommended, a philosopher and clergyman, Henry Philip Tappan. He had studied in Europe. He was known to have important ideas about education. Inquiries were made, and he was asked to take the job.

Well, Tappan said, he had no interest in presiding over a training school for ministers and schoolteachers, the mission of most American colleges of the day. His idea was larger.

"In our country we have no universities," Tappan wrote. "A University is literally a Cyclopedia where . . . in libraries, cabinets, apparatus, and professors, provision is made for carrying forward all scientific investigation; where study may be extended without limit, where the mind may be cultivated according to its wants. . . .

"Universities may, indeed, make learned men; but their best commendation is given when . . . they inspire men . . . to make themselves both

The Michigan campus in 1855, as depicted by painter Jasper Cropsey. Image: Jasper Francis Cropsey visual materials, Bentley Historical Library

learned and wise, and thus ready to put their hand to every great and good work, whether of science, of religion, or of the state."

In the 1850s, only one nation in the world had universities like that—Prussia, the biggest and strongest of the German principalities.

But Prussia was an authoritarian monarchy. Could a democratic republic build such a university?

Tappan believed it could and should, but only if the public supported it. Professors not only would spread existing knowledge by teaching. By deep study and research, they also would make new knowledge. They would train advanced students to push knowledge onward, generation after generation. And the purpose of all of it would be to serve the broadest public good.

No one knew where the free pursuit of knowledge would lead. That was the adventure of it.

But was that what Michigan wanted?

A Promising Start

Yes, Tappan was told, come west—build the school you have in mind here.

So he came, and of course he brought his wife: Julia Livingston Tappan.

"Livingston?" people asked. *Those* Livingstons?

Most Michiganians had been born in the East. They knew the Livingstons were one of the oldest and wealthiest families in New York state. And yes, Mrs. Tappan was one of those Livingstons. So when she said she and her husband were "missionaries to the West," as if their job were to civilize the wild frontier, people frowned.

Nonetheless, Tappan pressed ahead with his work, and if his wife offended some, his plans inspired others.

First the University must have more books, he urged, and collections of plants and animals and minerals to study, and the best scientific instruments.

A prominent and wealthy lawyer from Detroit, Henry Nelson Walker, asked how he could help.

Talk to your friends in the city, Tappan told Walker. Ask them to give money for a world-class astronomical observatory. A great telescope on the western frontier would send a signal of Michigan's serious intentions.

There was also a purely practical purpose, as Walker well

knew. He represented railroads, so he knew that observatories could give the precisely accurate measurements of time that railroads needed.

Walker gave $4,000, and he helped Tappan raise $11,000 more from other Detroiters. Tappan promised to name the new observatory in their honor. It was a highly promising start.

But Tappan's remarks about Prussian universities—and perhaps Mrs. Tappan's remarks about the uncivilized West—had attracted the jaundiced eye of Wilbur Fisk Storey, the new owner and editor of the *Detroit Free Press.*

He was a bad man to have as an enemy.

Blood Sport in Detroit

Storey had grown up angry. He quit school in Vermont at the age of 12—nothing unusual in the 1800s—and became a printer's apprentice. At 17 he took his trade west, where he became a newspaperman. But like most newspapermen of the day, he was really a printer just looking for ways to make money. Out of the back of his print shop he also sold drugs—the legal kind—and he cheated to get a big printing contract from the state government in Lansing.

He started a paper in Jackson, the *Patriot.* Then, soon after Henry Tappan arrived in Michigan, Storey took over the *Free Press* in Detroit. He said it would be "radically Democratic," a voice for the common-man tradition of Andrew Jackson.

He pumped up circulation with headlines like these:

HOW TO GET RID OF A FAITHLESS WIFE
DEATH IN THE BRIDAL BED
SAVED BY HIS WIFE'S CORPSE

Storey's own wife divorced him. An enemy editor said he frequented "dens of debauchery." A *Free Press* reporter said Storey "could say meaner things in fewer words than any person I ever saw." And in an era when newspapering was a blood sport, Storey made his name as the meanest public brawler in Michigan.

In the pages of the *Free Press,* his favorite targets were African-Americans, abolitionists and rival editors, one of whom he called "a living, moving gangrene in the eyes of the community—a stench to the nostrils of decency."

View of the Michigan University from the North East

The campus in 1854, from the vantage point of the future Detroit Observatory. Image: Adeline B. Mead Collection, Bentley Historical Library

That was Storey's normal style, and it sold papers. As one observer put it, "He commanded the admiration of an unthinking public which enjoyed his savage diatribes as they would have enjoyed a dog-fight."

He hadn't been in Detroit long when he spotted a perfect target.

Storey said the new university president in Ann Arbor—this New York snob who had married into the Livingston clan—was speaking far too admiringly of Europe. When Tappan praised the universities of Prussia, Storey pointed out that Americans had rebelled against one monarchy and had no intention of imitating another.

When Tappan gave his title as "chancellor" of the University—a word used in the state's own constitution—Storey said "chancellor" was an aristocratic European title, "unwarrantable, ridiculous, and contemptible."

Smaller Democratic papers across the state picked up the scent.

Tappan was "an aristocrat of the most exclusive school," said the *Kalamazoo Gazette.*

"The people want a practical, economical, self-sustaining institution," wrote the *Centreville Chronicle,* "and if Mr. Tappan is not satisfied with that, the sooner he leaves 'these diggins', the better."

"Of all the imitations of English aristocracy, German mysticism, Prussian imperiousness, and Parisian nonsensities," wrote the *Lansing Journal,* "he is altogether the most un-Americanized—the most completely foreignized specimen of an abnormal Yankee, we have ever seen."

When Wilbur Storey learned that Tappan had hired an actual Prussian to run the new observatory, he sharpened his blade for a vicious new thrust.

"A Master-hand to Manage It"

All this time, the new Detroit Observatory had been rising on a hill northeast of the campus, where the horizon was clear in every direction.

Inside, workers built a massive tower—a "pier"—to hold the main telescope. The pier started 15 feet below the ground and rose to 30 feet above it.

All the way around that central pier, the workers left an inch of empty space between the pier and the building, so that no vibration in the building would disturb the astronomer's view.

On the ground floor they installed a solid slab for a second, smaller instrument called a meridian circle telescope. It would be used to calculate the exact time by tracking the passage of stars overhead. The time would then be sent by telegraph to Detroit and points east and west.

Tappan traveled by train to New York, where he commissioned the great telescope maker Henry Fitz to make a refracting telescope, the third largest in the world, to explore the heavens. Tappan then crossed the Atlantic to Europe, where, in Berlin, he bargained with Pistor and Martins, the world's leading maker of optical instruments, for a meridian circle telescope to measure astronomical time.

At the Royal Observatory in Berlin, Tappan met a young astronomer of 32 with "exceedingly lustrous dark eyes." The man's English was halting, but he remarked to Tappan that whoever was chosen to use the new Pistor and Martins telescope would be lucky indeed.

Tappan learned that the man was one of the most promising astronomers in the world, and he remembered the name: Franz Brünnow.

Back in the United States, Tappan offered the astronomer's post to one American, then another, but neither wanted to move so far west.

Then Tappan thought of Brünnow in Berlin. He had no qualms about naming a European to Michigan's faculty, saying the Observatory "required a master-hand to manage it."

Brünnow accepted Tappan's offer. (He was the first Michigan professor to hold a Ph.D.) He went to work with the new telescopes, and before long Ann Arborites were seeing the young scientist in the company of the Tappans' daughter, Rebecca, known to everyone in town as Barbie. A love affair was beginning.

But in Detroit, Wilbur Storey was ready to make his new attack.

Tappan's Retort

Storey told readers of the *Free Press* that events in Ann Arbor had now gone far beyond "Prussianizing free Americans." The post of University astronomer had been given to a man "with whom . . . 'Chancellor' Tappan slept while contracting . . . for an astronomical clock." Now, Storey snickered, the two would be able "to once more sleep in the same bed."

Storey's poisonous attack backfired. Tappan's allies across the state were outraged. They rejected Storey's libel, praised the president's plans for the University, and defended him as a champion of democratic education.

"The Prussian system thus far has worked most admirably," a supporter wrote to Storey, "and the course of our institution is onward and upward. Look at these matters candidly, Mr. Editor. . . . He who attacks one whom the people love and respect—one to whom they are grateful—will sooner or later incur the popular displeasure and anathema."

Tappan told the legislature he had used the term "chancellor" with no Prussian connotation. He confessed that when criticized, he had stuck to "chancellor" out of sheer Dutch obstinacy. But he would happily drop it, he said, if the legislators would give him the tools to make the University great.

Wilbur Storey, apparently brought up short by Tappan's

defenders, eased off on the University and went off in search of new scandals.

In Ann Arbor, Franz Brünnow studied the heavens by night and courted Barbie Tappan by day. In 1857, three years after his arrival in Ann Arbor, the two were married, much to the approval of the bride's father. "Two beings never seemed happier," he remarked.

Seeds of Rancor

But Wilbur Storey had planted seeds of rancor against Tappan that sprouted and spread. By the early 1860s, the president was under fire from churchmen, legislators, and a new slate of regents.

In 1863, he was forced out of the presidency. He and his wife left the country to settle in Switzerland. The Brünnows soon followed.

But in Ann Arbor, a brilliant student of Brünnow's, James Craig Watson, assumed the astronomer's post and built on Brünnow's foundation. It was soon generally understood that the University of Michigan was the finest training ground for astronomers in the United States.

Tappan was gone. But his ideas had taken root.

"The Largest Figure of a Man"

Wilbur Storey left Detroit in 1861 to take over the *Chicago Times.* He survived the Civil War, padded his fortune, and died rich and despised.

In Ann Arbor, James Burrill Angell, appointed president of the University in 1871, took on the work of making Tappan's vision come fully to life. He would serve until 1909. In that time, departments of literature, science and the arts would multiply. Graduate programs and professional schools would train hundreds, then thousands.

The Detroit Observatory had been the first building on the campus devoted to research. Now it was followed by libraries, laboratories, and museums.

People began to see the observatory as the nucleus of what Tappan had envisioned—a new kind of American university, dedicated to the cultivation of every field of knowledge.

A statue of Henry Philip Tappan, by sculptor Karl Bitter, housed in Tappan Hall. Image: University of Michigan Photographs Vertical File, Bentley Historical Library

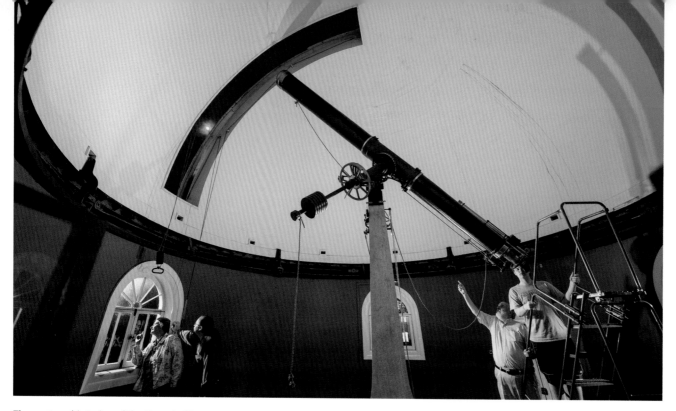

The restored interior of the Detroit Observatory.
Image: Eric Bronson, Michigan Photography

"I cannot speak of the Observatory without emotion," Tappan wrote. "No one will deny that it was a creation of my own."

If he had lost the battle for his own presidency, Tappan had, in the end, won the war for his grand design.

"Tappan was the largest figure of a man that ever appeared on the Michigan campus," Angell wrote, "and he was stung to death by gnats."

In 1875, as the University gained broad recognition as a leader in education, the regents officially expressed their regret over Tappan's ouster and offered their "full recognition of the great work done by him in organizing and constructing this institution of learning upon the basis from which its present prosperity has grown."

He was invited to Ann Arbor for commencement exercises. He declined. He never returned to the United States, and he died in 1881.

For decades the University grew up around the Observatory—the Medical Campus to the north, the Central Campus to the south and southwest. Larger telescopes were acquired. The Detroit Observatory grew old, fell into neglect, and was abandoned to use for storage.

In the late 1990s, the building was repaired, refurbished and reopened as a University museum.

And the telescopes that Henry Tappan had commissioned 150 years earlier were pointed at the sky again.

THIS IS MICHIGAN

GROUNDED IN SCIENCE. As U-M's first president, Henry Philip Tappan grounded the University's teaching and research in rigorous science—a bold commitment that shaped all of American education, particularly graduate education. Tappan's vision led to Michigan transforming research with many pioneering moments in higher education, including being the first university with a chemical laboratory (1856); first to own and operate its own hospital (1869); first public university with dental (1875) and pharmacy (1876) schools; first to teach aeronautical engineering (1914); and first with a program in human genetics (1940).

Researching specimens at the Museum of Zoology. Image: Eric Bronson, Michigan Photography

"He met both teacher and student alike in such a way as to put them at once at ease, and to make us feel that we were meeting not a superior but an equal and a friend."

—MARTIN D'OOGE, PROFESSOR OF GREEK

AN UNCOMMON LEADER

By James Tobin

University rules in the mid-1800s required students to attend chapel first thing every morning. But by tradition, chapel was a melee. In the big auditorium of the Law Building, just north of where Angell Hall stands now, a thousand students, most of them farm boys, yelled, pounded their feet, and pelted each other with anything handy, usually apple cores and walnuts. This had been going on for 20 years, and no president had been able to do anything about it. Professors had quit attending out of disgust.

James Burrill Angell had heard about chapel at Michigan even before he got to Ann Arbor in the summer of 1871. He had just left the presidency of the University of Vermont to take over at U-M, though only after he played hard to get for more than a year; he finally said yes when the Board of Regents agreed to his demand for an annual salary of $4,500.

On the first day of the term, Angell attended chapel and watched the usual small riot from the sidelines.

The next morning he came early, just as some sophomores were piling up ammo to throw at freshmen. Angell asked them—"kindly but firmly," he said later—not to throw stuff. They looked at him—and dropped their nuts under their chairs.

The following day the new president conducted prayers himself and made a few general remarks about rowdiness in chapel. He did it with "a cherubic smile and an appeal to [the

President James Burrill Angell in 1879. Image: Sam B. Revenaugh, Bentley Historical Library

Opposite page: View of University of Michigan's campus circa 1873, two years after the arrival of President James Burrill Angell. Image: University of Michigan Photographs Vertical File, Bentley Historical Library

students'] sense of fair play." And that was that. Rowdiness at chapel was over.

Why So Easy?

People said there was just something about Angell.

"The kindliness of his manner and the gentleness of his words were sometimes mistaken for weakness and acquiescence," said Martin D'Ooge, a professor of Greek who watched Angell in the presidency for many years. "Not until they felt the firm grip of the strong and determined will did the boys learn to know that his words, spoken ever so gently, could not be lightly disregarded."

And he met people halfway, as students soon learned. Angell led the prayers at chapel every morning. But he made chapel voluntary.

"He met both teacher and student alike in such a way as to put them at once at ease," D'Ooge said, "and to make us feel that we were meeting not a superior but an equal and a friend."

A Man of Conviction

Born in Scituate, Rhode Island, in 1829, Angell was descended from a friend and fellow traveler of Roger Williams, the New England rebel who championed religious freedom against the Puritans. Angell was so brilliant as a student at Brown University that the faculty recruited him to join their ranks. He did for a while, then became editor of the *Providence Journal*, where he was a strong backer of Abraham Lincoln.

When the Civil War ended Angell returned to academe. After several years at Vermont, he responded to the challenge of building up the still shaky public university in the West. He spoke with a Yankee twang, and it took him a while to set aside a belief in New England's cultural primacy. But he made friends and allies immediately, and he got to work on the project of turning a great experiment—that is, the notion of a world-class university supported by public means—into a practical reality.

Angell's mixture of good fellowship and a strong will made him the most influential of Michigan's presidents. He served until 1909—38 years in which U-M expanded from three departments to seven; the faculty grew from 35 to some 250; and enrollment rose from about 1,000 students to more than 4,000. By the time he retired, Michigan was easily the leading public university in the country.

An Open Mind

Angell revolutionized the curriculum, replacing the old system by which every student took virtually the same course of study with a new system heavy on electives. That not only gave students freedom to study what they wanted; it also led to a spectacular diversification of course offerings. And that led, in turn, to a faculty of top-tier minds in many fields, from John Dewey in philosophy to Frederick Novy in bacteriology.

"The most striking feature of the University," *Harper's Magazine* said in 1887, "is the broad and liberal spirit in which it does its work. Students are allowed the widest freedom consistent with sound scholarship in pursuing the studies of their choice; they are held to no minute police regulations, but are treated as persons with high and definite aims, from which they are not to be easily diverted."

For most of his tenure Angell wrote his own letters by hand; he personally registered every student enrolling in the Department of Literature, Science, and the Arts; and he taught courses in international law. (U.S. presidents sent him on foreign missions; his tours of duty led to U-M's special ties with China and the Philippines.) Michigan's first women students started just when Angell became president. He supported them and became a strong advocate of coeducation.

An Uncommon Education

In Angell's time, college was widely seen as the elite sphere of the wealthy. He was determined to have Michigan break that mold. In the 1880s he did his own study to find that the fathers of nearly half of U-M students earned a living with their hands, and fewer than one in four had a college degree. He pitched Michigan on that basis, and thereby established U-M's reputation as a democratic, egalitarian place offering what has become known as "an uncommon education for the common man" and woman.

"Dear Old Prexy," a retired James Burrill Angell in 1912, as captured in the scrapbook of a student. Image: E.C. Morris, Rena Marguerite Lundell scrapbook, Bentley Historical Library

"Have an aristocracy of birth if you will," he said, "or of riches if you wish, but give our plain boys from the log cabins a chance to develop their minds with the best learning and we fear nothing from your aristocracy."

He also insisted that students who enjoyed the benefits of a public-supported education owed society something in return—and that their public service in turn justified public support. He would tell the story of a doctor trained at U-M who was called out in the middle of the night to save the child of a poor family. "Who is reaping the greatest benefit from the education he has gained here," Angell asked, "the physician, with or without his scanty fee, or the anxious parents to whom he has restored the child from the jaws of death?"

In his final baccalaureate address in 1909, Angell told his last class of graduating seniors: "We have a right to ask, and we do ask, the University asks, the state asks of every one of you, that your life be shaped on a larger and fairer pattern because you have been here."

Angell died in 1916 at 87. One of his sons became president of Yale; another became professor of law at Michigan; a grandson became U-M's chair of sociology; and a granddaughter won the Pulitzer Prize in history.

THIS IS MICHIGAN

A BOLD EXPERIMENT. Women were admitted starting with Madelon Stockwell in 1870, the first for a large state university. The first African-American woman in the country to earn a degree in dentistry—Ida Gray—did so at U-M in 1890. Forty years after women first were admitted, they outnumbered men being inducted into the Phi Beta Kappa honor society. Notable alumnae include Alice Freeman Palmer, named to the presidency of Wellesley College in 1882, who quickly became the nation's leading advocate of higher education for women; longtime U.S. Sen. Nancy Landon Kassebaum; and Dr. Antonia Novello, first woman and first Hispanic to serve as U.S. surgeon general.

Alumna Antonia Novello speaks at Winter Commencement in 1994. Image: Michigan Photography

RADICAL NEW THINKERS
Origins of a Reputation

By Francis X. Blouin Jr.

When you look at the famous Jasper Cropsey painting of the University of Michigan campus in 1855, you cannot help but be struck by how isolated the place was. There are only a few buildings evident. Cows are grazing in a meadow. And we know that Ann Arbor was a small town of some 4,500 people. How did that place, then, become, within a span of 50 years, one of the most important intellectual centers in the nation? What is the origin of Michigan's reputation?

There are many answers. By 1880, the University of Michigan was one of a handful of institutions of higher education positioned to rise to the highest levels of intellectual achievement. This was not on the coattails of any group of institutions—because none preceded it. It was a time of intellectual transformation in the nation as a whole—and Michigan, along with Harvard, Yale, Princeton, Johns Hopkins and later Chicago were positioned to seize a moment.

And they did. It was the presence of a handful of men (alas in those days, only men) on Michigan's campus who were informed by, and contributed to, discussions on how to construct and categorize knowledge. Central to their work were debates over the relevance of science and religion, over how we understand man as a moral and social being, and finally the broader applications of science to that understanding.

The campus in 1946.
Image: News and Information Services Collection, Bentley Historical Library

Education and Moral Man

Up until the late 19th century, especially in the United States, the province of human behavior—of moral man—was considered inextricably bound to a moral authority rooted in the Bible. If the world was not flat and not created in seven real days, it still was generally accepted that religion explained humans and human relationships.

Education, then, was the means to prepare the moral man. With few exceptions (Michigan being one) colleges and universities established before the Morrill Act of 1863 were founded on religion. This central role would only be challenged (particularly in the United States) seriously, systematically and fundamentally, in the late-19th century.

Charles Darwin's proposition on the origin of species had a profound influence on intellectual life, and consequently on higher education. However, some of his side points grabbed particular attention: the ideas of randomness, of biological organism, that species adapt and change, and that patterns in natural development are observable. Combined with ideas from the emerging field of social psychology, Darwin's theories suggested that how we know and how we act is biological, not spiritual. It was bold and distinctly not biblical: We as individuals are organisms and society itself is an organism composed of organisms.

Henry Philip Tappan came to U-M as president in 1852 to transform it into a rigorous intellectual center on the Prussian model. Tappan's sympathies were very clearly with emerging notions of science. We see that in the people he hired, such as Andrew Dickson White and Alexander Winchell, as well as in his work to establish a campus observatory. While Tappan's arrival predated Darwin's book, his actions were important because he boldly moved Michigan toward science and scientific investigation.

Establishing this scientific environment was one thing, but fully realizing its potential was quite another. Enter James B. Angell with his capable and perceptive leadership.

The Angell Influence

As U-M's third president, Angell embraced new ways of thinking, and moved to hire several key scholars who would put Michigan at the very center of the idea of the research university.

Among the appointments was John Dewey, a junior professor of philosophy who argued that instead of thinking of ourselves exclusively as a creation of a higher power, we are ourselves our own creation—in how we understand our self, how we understand our self in relationship to others, and how others perceive us. The individual and the environment are connected, he argued, asking the deeper question, If we shape ourselves, can we be changed by ourselves?

George Herbert Mead was another who came to U-M and argued that the emergence of the mind depends upon interaction between the total human organism and its social environment. Refining Mead's views further was yet another Angell appointee, social theorist Charles Horton Cooley. He emphasized that the study of social relations required its own discipline with special attention to the implications for social improvement.

A fourth hire, Henry Carter Adams, took these ideas and adapted them to an understanding of the behavior of the social economy. He argued that just as social interactions could be studied and encouraged to better ends, so too could economic behavior be studied and, where necessary, regulated for the improvement of society as a whole.

Guided by Angell, Michigan was forging a community of radical new thinkers who created one of the most important intellectual environments of the early 20th century. Through Dewey and his ideas of self, society, and education; through Mead and his ideas on the capacity of societies to achieve social transformation; through Cooley and his ideas for the study of social processes; and through Adams and his confidence in ways to reshape capitalist economies, Michigan would lay the ground for new conceptions of education, research and knowledge itself.

The Modern University

Scholars at Michigan, along with those at a handful of other institutions, were posing fundamentally new ideas about human nature and the social order. It was among the first institutions to apply ideas and methodologies of science to social issues. This was, and is, social science.

Select faculty members at Harvard, Yale, Johns Hopkins, Princeton, Michigan, Wisconsin, and later Cornell, and the newer universities at Berkeley, Stanford, and Chicago, transformed the intellectual ambitions of higher education. They developed a new structure of how we approach knowledge and how we address the challenges of a complex society. These universities were among the 14 founders of the Association of American Universities that in 1900 came together to define the modern American research university, a model that is still with us today.

THIS IS MICHIGAN

HIGHER ED LEADERSHIP. Michigan was a founding member of the Association of American Universities, formed in 1900 by the leading Ph.D.-granting institutions of the day to elevate America's academic quality and reputation. This leadership in higher education is reflected in the numerous U-M alumni and faculty who have served as university presidents and chancellors. Michigan graduates and faculty have led such prestigious institutions as Northwestern (Erastus Haven), Wisconsin (Charles Kendall Adams), MIT (Charles M. Vest) and more. In the 21st century, some of America's most notable universities, including Columbia University, the University of Virginia, Dartmouth College, Syracuse University and Oberlin College, were being led by women and men shaped by Michigan.

Alumnus James Rowland Angell,
president of Yale University.
Image: Manuscripts & Archives,
Yale University

Alumna Alice Freeman Palmer,
president of Wellesley College.
Image: Library of Congress, Rare Book
and Special Collections Division

University of Michigan—Flint

We must answer the question: Is the University of Michigan a geographic fact or is it a mission, a program, a concept of education, a kingdom of the mind and of the spirit? To the extent that we have engaged in extension, resident graduate centers, and so forth, we have partially answered that it is not geography, but purpose and accomplishment. We are now asked to consider a firmer commitment to the broader concept. Shall we establish Flint College of the University of Michigan?

—PRESIDENT HARLAN H. HATCHER, 1955

1950: The voters of Flint and philanthropist Charles Stewart Mott agree to commit several million dollars toward higher education in their city.

1955: The U-M Board of Regents approves the concept of a two-year senior college in Flint.

1956: Classes begin with 167 students at what is known as the Flint College of the University of Michigan, led by Dean David French.

1958: The first class graduates in ceremonies in Ann Arbor.

1965: Flint College becomes a four-year college.

1970: The North Central Association of Colleges and Schools accredits Flint College.

1971: Flint College becomes the University of Michigan—Flint, with William E. Moran appointed chancellor.

1972: Regents purchase 42 acres of land for a campus along the Flint River.

1980: Conny Nelson is named chancellor.

1984: Clinton Jones is appointed chancellor.

1990: UM-Flint extends downtown by purchasing the abandoned Water Street Pavilion.

1994: Charlie Nelms is appointed chancellor.

1999: Juan Mestas becomes chancellor.

2000: Alumnus Christopher Paul Curtis, author of *Bud, Not Buddy,* becomes the first African-American man to win the Newbery Medal for excellence in children's literature.

2002: The William S. White Building opens on the site of the former AutoWorld theme park.

2008: First Street Residence Hall opens as the first student housing.

2008: Ruth J. Person becomes chancellor, the first woman to hold the position.

2010: UM-Flint receives the Community Engagement Classification from the Carnegie Foundation for the Advancement of Teaching.

Image: Scott Galvin Photography

2013: UM-Flint offers its first doctorate, a Ph.D. in physical therapy.

2014: Susan E. Borrego becomes UM-Flint's seventh chancellor.

2015: The campus footprint grows by 25 percent with the purchase of the First Merit Bank building and the donation of the Riverfront Residence Hall and Banquet Center.

2016: The campus celebrates its 60th anniversary, with an enrollment of approximately 8,600.

University of Michigan—Dearborn

It is increasingly evident that our nation is extremely short of facilities necessary for the needs of higher education, particularly in Engineering and Business Administration. Such a shortage is of major concern to Michigan, where the prosperity of the State is so dependent upon an adequate supply of engineering skills and industrial leadership. . . . Dearborn has a center of high population concentration, a rich supply, in quality and quantity, of industrial sources for cooperative programs in Engineering and in Business Administration and there are large tracts of vacant land ideally suited as sites of educational institutions.

—U-M INTERNAL MEMO, 1958

1956: Ford Motor Company donates $6.5 million and 202 acres to U-M for a branch campus in Dearborn. The land includes portions of inventor Henry Ford's estate.

1959: The Dearborn Center of the University of Michigan opens, offering upper-level classes. Thirty-four students enroll under the direction of William E. Stirton.

1963: Dearborn Center becomes the Dearborn Campus.

1964: The first graduate program, a master of science in mechanical engineering, is offered.

1967: Fair Lane, the Henry Ford residence on the Dearborn campus, becomes a National Historic Landmark.

1968: Norman R. Scott is named dean of Dearborn Campus.

1969: Dearborn Campus becomes a four-year college.

1970: The North Central Association of Colleges and Schools accredits UM-Dearborn Campus.

1971: UM-Dearborn Campus becomes the University of Michigan—Dearborn.

1971: Leonard E. "Pat" Goodall is appointed the first chancellor.

1974: The first varsity sport—soccer—is offered.

1977: Athletics teams are officially named the Wolves.

1980: William A. Jenkins is named chancellor.

1982: The first Honors Convocation takes place.

1988: Blenda Wilson is named chancellor, becoming the first African-American woman to be an executive officer of the University of Michigan.

1993: James C. Rennick is inaugurated as chancellor.

2000: Daniel E. Little is named UM-Dearborn's fifth chancellor.

2010: Economics alumna Rima Fakih is the first Arab-American woman to be named Miss USA.

2012: UM-Dearborn awards its first doctorate—a Ph.D. in automotive systems engineering.

2012: The Union at Dearborn, a privately owned housing facility for students, opens adjacent to campus.

2015: The Carnegie Foundation for the Advancement of Teaching awards its Community Engagement Classification to UM-Dearborn.

2015: Chancellor Little begins his fourth term, making him the longest-serving chancellor in campus history.

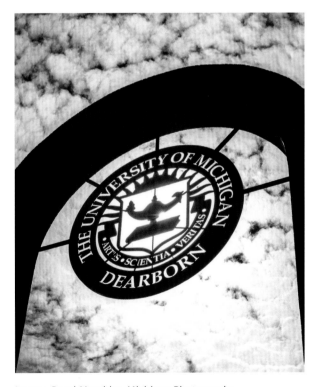

Image: Daryl Marshke, Michigan Photography

PERSONALITIES

"Without permission from anyone, I began planting trees within the University enclosure; established, on my own account, several avenues; and set out elms to overshadow them."

—PROFESSOR ANDREW DICKSON WHITE

PROFESSOR WHITE'S TREES

By James Tobin

The Ann Arbor campus was barely 20 years old when Andrew Dickson White first saw it. Just married, he arrived from Yale in October 1857 to teach history and English literature. He was only 24, the youngest member of the faculty, and he looked even younger. In fact, a student at the train station mistook him for an entering freshman and showed him all the way into town before realizing the newcomer was a professor.

It was the time of year when Michigan's leaves are aflame in yellow and red, and White's first impression as he entered the village, he wrote later, was of "a beautiful place." But he saw one glaring drawback.

"The 'campus' on which stood the four buildings then devoted to instruction, greatly disappointed me," he later wrote. "It was a flat, square inclosure of forty acres, unkempt and wretched. Throughout its whole space there were not more than a score of trees outside the building sites allotted to professors; unsightly plank walks connected the buildings, and in every direction were meandering paths, which in dry weather were dusty and in wet weather muddy. Coming, as I did, from the glorious elms of Yale, all this distressed me."

A scrubby field was no fit place for learning, and he was not going to leave it that way.

Andrew Dickson White about 1865. Image: Division of Rare and Manuscript Collections, Cornell University Library

Young elms grow along Diag walkways laid out by Professor White. At right, in the background, is the rear of the President's House. Image: University of Michigan Photographs Vertical File, Bentley Historical Library

A campus visitor, Will Caine, feeds a Diag friend in 1909. Image: Courtesy of Barry LaRue

A Personal Project

White asked around: Why so few trees?

Well, people said, it wasn't that no one had tried.

In the early '50s, Dr. Edmund Andrews, who doubled as professor of anatomy and superintendent of grounds, had rounded up some citizens and students for a program to plant a thousand trees. But most of the seedlings died. People said the ground was too hard and dry.

White didn't believe it. In the village blocks west of the campus, he saw plenty of "fine large trees, and among them elms" growing in "the little inclosures about the pretty cottages."

White decided the problem must have been lack of proper care. So, with neither permission nor funding, he took matters into his own hands.

First, he observed the human geography—the paths that students had created simply by walking between buildings. The fashion in landscape design just then was to create outdoor corridors shrouded in green canopies. This was the effect White wanted. So he marked off several walkways—including, apparently, the basic X of the Diag—and set to work.

"The Light of History"

"Without permission from anyone," he would write in his autobiography, "I began planting trees within the University enclosure; established, on my own account, several avenues; and set out elms to overshadow them. Choosing my trees with care, carefully protecting and watering them . . . and gradually adding to them a considerable number of evergreens, I preached practically the doctrine of adorning the campus. Gradually some of my students joined me; one class after another aided in securing trees and in planting them, others became interested, until, finally, the University authorities made me 'superintendent of the grounds,' and appropriated to my work the munificent sum of seventy-five dollars a year."

Not that White was neglecting the work he had been hired for.

His devotion to history had arisen as the Northern and

Southern states approached a collision in their long dispute over slavery. White was an abolitionist, but he felt a particular calling apart from politics. "Though I felt deeply the importance of the questions then before the country," he wrote, "it seemed to me the only way in which I could contribute anything to their solution was in aiding to train up a new race of young men who should understand our own time and its problems in the light of history."

After graduating from Yale, he took more training in Berlin and Paris, then returned to New Haven for a master's degree. In American colleges very few courses were devoted solely to history, and most classes consisted of droning recitations out of textbooks. But in Europe, White heard professors give sparkling talks that treated history as "a living subject having relations to present questions." He thought he might do the same in America.

The question was where he would do this work—in the East, or somewhere new.

Elms planted by Andrew Dickson White in the 1850s and '60s still dominated the Diag in the 1930s. Image: Ivory Photo Collection, Bentley Historical Library

"Hardy, Vigorous, Shrewd"

Friends who heard White's ideas about teaching urged him to stay in the East and join the faculty at Yale. But on the day of his commencement as a master's candidate, he heard an address by President Francis Wayland of Brown University, who told the graduates: "The best field of work for graduates now is in the West; our country is shortly to arrive at a switching-off place for good or evil. [He meant the coming clash between North and South.] Our Western states are to hold the balance of power in the Union, and to determine whether the country shall become a blessing or a curse in human history."

"I had never seen him before," White wrote. "I never saw him afterward. His speech lasted ten minutes, but it settled a great question for me. I went home [to upstate New York] and wrote to sundry friends that I was a candidate for the profes-

Summer in the Diag. ca. 1937. Image: University of Michigan Photographs Vertical File, Bentley Historical Library

sorship of history in any Western college where there was a chance to get at students, and as a result received two calls—one to a Southern university, which I could not accept on account of my anti-slavery opinions; the other to the University of Michigan, which I accepted."

It was a very good match. Michigan's president, Henry Philip Tappan, spotted White as just the sort of bright young scholar who could help fulfill Tappan's vision of a citadel of higher learning dedicated to the public good. White's students liked him and he returned their respect. They were "worth teaching," he said, "hardy, vigorous, shrewd, broad, with faith in the greatness of the country and enthusiasm regarding the nation's future. . . .

"I soon became intensely interested in my work, and looked forward to it every day with pleasure."

And when classes were over for the day, Professor White went outside to check on his trees.

"Splendid Growth"

For two years he nursed his seedlings. He pruned them and protected them from insects. In the heat of summer he made sure they had enough water. They survived, then thrived and grew.

Students began to join him. Young men soon to board trains for Southern battlefields went out to the woods around Ann Arbor and returned with seedlings. Two nurserymen from New York sent a gift of 60 trees that were planted in a grove near the northern edge of the central grounds. The class of 1858 placed 50 young maples in concentric circles around the great native oak. White added more maples along one side of the fence that bordered State Street on the west. The literary faculty donated 42 elms for the other side of the street.

"So began the splendid growth that now surrounds those buildings."

White tended the trees, taught his students, and began the research and writing that would make him one of the leading American historians of his generation. Then, in the spring of 1861, the Civil War began, "and there came a great exodus of students into the armies," he wrote, "the vast majority taking up arms for the Union, and a few for the Confederate States. The very noblest of them thus went forth—many of them, alas,

Following page: The Diag in 1947. Image: News and Information Services Collection, Bentley Historical Library

45

"This is the heart of a great university; warm, tranquil, peaceful, democratic. It is one of the things worth preserving."

never to return, and among them not a few whom I loved as brothers and even as my own children."

As the war approached its climax, White's father died, and he had to go home to manage his family's business affairs. Almost immediately he was elected to the New York state legislature. In 1865 he co-founded Cornell University and became its first president.

For a number of years he retained a lectureship at Michigan and returned periodically to teach, but after a while his duties in Ithaca made that impossible.

But those trees in Ann Arbor remained "to me as my own children."

"More Trees Than Boys"

White was president of Cornell until 1885; U.S. ambassador to Germany from 1879 to 1881; minister to Russia from 1892 to 1894; president of the American Historical Association; and president of the American Social Science Association. As the 20th century began he continued to write and speak widely.

Down through the decades of his long life, he returned to Ann Arbor from time to time to see friends and give lectures. He always visited his trees. On one visit, he was seen out on the Diag at night, going from tree to tree with a lantern.

At Cornell in the spring of 1911, he had a sudden whim. From his papers he pulled out an old map, then boarded the train for Ann Arbor.

The next day, on the Diag, a student recognized the old man walking slowly from tree to tree, looking from his map to the trees. The student asked him what he was doing.

"Yesterday," he said, "while sitting in my library at Ithaca, I happened to think that fifty years ago today the class of 1861 planted these trees under my direction. I had among my papers a plot of the ground, the location of each tree and the name of the student who planted it."

He gestured at the trees and said: "There are more trees alive than boys."

On the Diag

The beauty of the Diag is improvisational. It is less elegant than a formal landscape design, but more comfortable, even homey, partly because the trees have been planted piecemeal. They were planted here and there as buildings came and went and as walkways changed, creating a particular sense of place that has changed over time, but only gradually, so that each generation has had its own Diag, slightly different from the Diag of the generation before and after.

In 1940, when the nation was preparing for its all but inevitable entry into World War II, an anonymous writer captured the feelings of a moment at the center of the campus:

"A warm summer day has given way to a perfect summer night, overcast but with a quarter-moon breaking through the clouds above the campus trees. It is a few minutes past nine as you swing onto the Diagonal. The darkness insulates you, the air is caressing; you move almost effortlessly under the long aisle of trees. It is quiet except for the insistent cheeping of insects among the leaves, and occasional distant voices. . . .

"This is the heart of a great university; warm, tranquil, peaceful, democratic. It is one of the things worth preserving."

In 2014, a bur oak was given by students, faculty and staff to commemorate the inauguration of Mark S. Schlissel as Michigan's 14th president. If all goes well, it will grow tall in the northwest corner of the Diag, about where Andrew Dickson White stood when he first saw the campus.

WALLENBERG AT MICHIGAN

By Kim Clarke

Before made all the difference. Before outfoxing the Nazis, risking his life, and saving 100,000 Jews from the hell of World War II death camps. Before living on the run and being the target of assassins. Before disappearing into a Russian gulag and being forever silenced.

Before the statues, the streets bearing his name, and the global tributes exalting his bravery and sacrifice. Before becoming the only person other than Winston Churchill to be made an honorary U.S. citizen.

Before all this, Raoul Wallenberg was a University of Michigan student.

Days removed from an ocean liner that carried him from his native Sweden, he walked onto the Ann Arbor campus in 1931 much like any freshman: eager to fit in and succeed.

If one indeed believes leaders are not born, but are made, then Michigan helped make Wallenberg. And his days in Ann Arbor would shape a brand of heroism that distinguished Raoul Wallenberg, Class of 1935, as one of the 20th century's most extraordinary humanitarians.

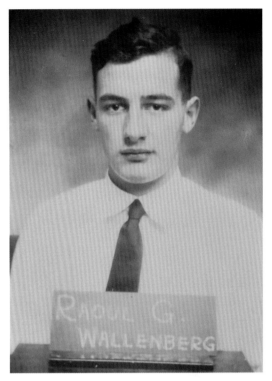

Raoul Wallenberg at U-M freshman registration. Image: Raoul Wallenberg Vertical File, Bentley Historical Library

The Classmate

Enrolling at Michigan was largely the decision of Wallenberg's grandfather and mentor, Gustaf Wallenberg. Raoul was his only grandson, and that Gustaf adored him was an understatement.

Leonard Baskin's Holocaust memorial on Raoul Wallenberg Plaza, east of the Rackham School of Graduate Studies. Image: Paul Jaronski, Michigan Photography

> "His days in Ann Arbor would shape a brand of heroism that distinguished Raoul Wallenberg, Class of 1935, as one of the 20th century's most extraordinary humanitarians."

"You are the dearest thing I have on this earth," he told his grandson on his 20th birthday.

He wanted an American education for Raoul not for the coursework, which he felt could be equaled in Swedish universities, but rather for the lessons of living and learning in a new environment. Raoul, he believed, should absorb the confidence he associated with the United States.

Raoul Wallenberg was a child of wealth and privilege, born into a family that had built a banking and industrial empire unrivaled in Sweden. He was cosmopolitan; elitism was the family norm, as were global influence and connections.

His friends at Michigan knew none of this. He was, simply, Rudy Wallenberg.

He lived in plain boardinghouses ("I'm going to get another room for the summer because the one I have now is in an attic and I'm sure it will be insufferable"). He had no interest in fraternities, and little use for college pranks.

He would walk three blocks from his room on East Madison to have breakfast at the Michigan Union, enjoying grapefruit in the dining room before classes.

He sweated exams ("I feel totally exhausted") and felt the loneliness that envelops international students at the holidays. "Everybody leaves town within a few hours of the last classes before Christmas, and from then to the seventh of January the place is like a tomb. . . . Christmas Eve I felt rather lonely and gloomy."

Friends and faculty knew him as both mature beyond his years and a happy-go-lucky kid. A highlight of being an architecture student was an annual dance, with elaborate scenery and costumes plotted out months in advance by students. Attending his final ball, Wallenberg joined in the "Arabian Nights" theme he helped orchestrate.

He did not get overly excited about grades, awards or social status. What mattered most, he said, was the experience of living. "My school work has, on the whole, paid off not only when it comes to grades, because that isn't too important, but because I really feel that I've learned something."

The Traveler

Wallenberg did not sit still in Ann Arbor. He spent his summers on campus, taking courses that would allow him to

Within weeks of arriving from his native Sweden, Wallenberg settled into his first year of classes. Image: University of Michigan Necrology Files, Bentley Historical Library

graduate early. He went canoeing on nearby lakes. He bicycled; once, he pedaled 60 miles to Owosso to speak to a ladies' civic club about Sweden. The women celebrated his visit with "dainty refreshments," each topped with a tiny blue-and-yellow Swedish flag.

But he relished new sights and people different than himself. He traveled alone, with friends, and with his professors. He wanted to soak up what he saw as strictly American phenomena: hot dog stands, drugstores, newsreel theaters, air conditioning and more.

Visiting New York City, he was in awe of the newest skyscrapers: the Empire State Building and the Chrysler Building ("very beautiful . . . light and graceful"). In Chicago, he worked as a summer volunteer at the 1933 World's Fair.

He loved to hitchhike, a popular mode of transportation during the Depression. Not only did it save money—he boasted about thumbing his way from Ann Arbor to Los Angeles and not spending a dime—but hitchhiking was an adventure.

"You're in close contact with new people each and every day. Hitchhiking gives you training in diplomacy and tact."

Only once in his travels did he encounter trouble, when four men robbed and beat him on a road outside of Chicago. A gun was flashed and Wallenberg was thrown into a ditch.

It left him unfazed. "I found the whole thing sort of interesting," he told his mother. "This will not make me give up hitchhiking. I'll just carry less money on me and try to become more devious."

Raoul Wallenberg in his senior year at U-M.
Image: Bentley Historical Library

The Lover

Like so many before and after him, Wallenberg found a soul mate while a U-M student. Rather than pursuing a fellow classmate, however, he dated a young faculty member at Michigan State Normal College, now Eastern Michigan University, in neighboring Ypsilanti.

Bernice Ringman was a physiotherapist in the school's special education department. She was four years older than Wallenberg, who, within months of arriving in Ann Arbor, said he was struck by the poise of American women. "As a rule they are nice and quite knowledgeable. They also have more backbone than most of the men."

Wallenberg and Ringman undoubtedly bonded over his native Sweden. Her parents were Swedish immigrants, and as a teenager she had traveled to their homeland.

In Ann Arbor, the couple attended performances of Handel's "Messiah" every December in Hill Auditorium, as well as the annual architects' ball. It was only after Wallenberg graduated and returned to Europe that he learned Ringman had fallen in love with him; each letter to Stockholm carried more affection. It was a revelation that left Wallenberg both depressed and distressed. When Ringman sent a telegram on his 23rd birthday, asking if he loved her, he immediately wired back: No.

"I liked her so much and hated to know that I was the cause of her unhappiness."

Wallenberg shared this angst with his grandfather. The old man had repeatedly warned against romance. Women, he told his grandson, are hyenas who "use all means at their disposal to get their claws into whatever young man that suits their designs."

He was therefore apoplectic when his grandson poured out his heart about Ringman. Did you seduce her? Is she pregnant? "I fully realize how easily the sexual urges of a young man can lead to a liaison with a young girl, but he must not let them put his future at risk."

The reaction was so severe that Wallenberg dashed off an immediate telegram to put his grandfather at ease. *"Please dont [sic] worry/no complications/affection her part only."*

Neither Wallenberg nor Ringman would ever marry.

The Architect

More than anything, Wallenberg wanted to be an architect. By choosing Michigan, he was attending one of the premier American programs of its day.

Wallenberg arrived at an exhilarating moment for the program. Its leader, Professor Emil Lorch, had been at U-M for a quarter century and was determined to see architecture—then part of the College of Engineering—become an independent school in its own building. Michigan Architecture was one of the largest programs in the country, and it needed to make its mark.

The building came first, in 1928, a four-story brick structure designed by Lorch and located at what was then a far corner of campus. Three years later, with the blessing of the Board of

A student draws in the Architecture Building, today's Lorch Hall. Image: A. Alfred Taubman College of Architecture and Urban Planning Records, Bentley Historical Library

Regents, the College of Architecture was born, with Lorch as its first dean.

This was the environment that awaited Wallenberg. No doubt he appreciated the European flair of the faculty, with architects from Finland, Denmark, Austria and France among the teaching corps.

He designed restaurants and houses. Challenged to find ways to house thousands inexpensively, he spent 10 weeks devising an entire community, on paper. He was honest in saying he put his time and creativity into architecture at the expense of subjects he disliked, such as chemistry and math ("there is a real disaster brewing").

When he graduated in 1935, Wallenberg received the American Institute of Architects silver medal as Michigan's most outstanding student.

Even so, he was more artist than architect.

"Raoul Wallenberg was so apt a student in drawing and painting—I must have had him in three or four classes during his studies with us—that he got nothing but As from, I suppose, all of us. He definitely did from me," Jean Paul Slusser, a professor of drawing and painting, told an interviewer years later. "I asked him finally if he were not intending to be an artist. He looked at me slowly and, as I think of it now, perhaps a little sadly.

"He then explained to me briefly and with enormous modesty, too, who his family were and how the sons of the house of Wallenberg were educated."

That meant the world of banking and, as Wallenberg saw it, a career being "a commercial ditto." After graduating and landing business internships in South Africa and Palestine, he remained unsettled about his future.

"To tell you the truth, I don't find myself very bankerish: the director of a bank should be judgelike and calm and cold and cynical besides. . . . My temperament is better suited to some positive line of work than to sitting around saying no."

The Leader

Raoul Wallenberg was blessed with what his grandfather called "the wonderful gift of a cool head." His defiance in the face of Nazi brutality during World War II is a modern-day morality play. As a Swedish diplomat assigned in 1944 to Hungary—one

Raoul Wallenberg on the steps of Angell Hall.
Image: Raoul Wallenberg Photograph Vertical
File, Bentley Historical Library

of Europe's few remaining pockets of Jewish people—he made it a personal mission to disrupt Hitler's "Final Solution."

Using his gift for drawing, he created fake Swedish passports for Jews in Budapest. Distributed en masse, the cleverly designed but entirely bogus *Schutzpass* provided immediate diplomatic immunity.

He leaned on his urban planning lessons to develop safe houses, renting and reconfiguring apartment buildings to hold far more people than they were designed for and, in the process, providing a safe haven for Jews.

Where in the 1930s he partied in the costumes of the U-M Architects' Ball, in the war he disguised fair-haired Hungarian Jews in SS uniforms, seizing upon their Aryan looks to infiltrate the German troops. The impostors would free Jews, explaining they were captured by mistake.

He handed Jews a second chance at life, pulling them from rolling trains bound for concentration camps. When trains were no longer available and the Germans forced prisoners to march to the death camps, Wallenberg followed, shoving food, medicine and passports at the emaciated victims.

Dining with Adolf Eichmann, mastermind of the Nazi death camps, Wallenberg calmly told him: "Why don't you call off your people?" Eichmann had earlier branded Wallenberg "Jewdog" and directed German sharpshooters to kill him.

In the course of six months, Wallenberg rescued an estimated 100,000 people from the smoldering shell of Budapest. No other individual has been credited with saving so many from extinction.

Memorial commemorating Raoul Wallenberg, located in his native Sweden. Image: Karsten Ratzke. Creative Commons CC0 1.0

Raoul Wallenberg disappeared in 1945, taken by Russian troops into so-called protective custody and held in a Moscow prison. He was 32 and never heard from again.

Like Wallenberg's disappearance, the source of his moral courage is a mystery. What is known is that this humanitarian grew to maturity in Ann Arbor. "The years Raoul spent in America, studying at the University of Michigan and traveling around, were critical to the development of his character," his cousins Gustaf Söderlund and Gitte Wallenberg wrote nearly 50 years after he vanished.

When Wallenberg was approaching his senior year and the world was at peace, he voiced the melancholy that so many students experience as college draws to a close.

"I feel so at home in my little Ann Arbor that I am beginning to sink roots here and have a hard time imagining my leaving it. But I am not doing anything very useful here."

There were lives to save.

THIS IS MICHIGAN

ALUMNI IMPACT. The Michigan alumni body is the largest in the world. Graduates have made an impact in all arenas, from public service (Gerald R. Ford, Mary Frances Berry, H. Gardner Ackley) and technology (John Seely Brown, Clarence "Kelly" Johnson, Arthur W. Burks, Tony Fadell) to the arts (James Earl Jones, Leslie Bassett, Gilda Radner, Darren Criss), sciences (John Clark Sheehan, Antonia Novello, Samuel C.C. Ting, Alexa Canady) and sports (Janet Guthrie, William DeHart Hubbard, Micki King, Tom Brady). Branch Rickey helped integrate major league baseball and William Mayo co-founded the Mayo Clinic. Perhaps the most unique alumni achievement was the all-Michigan crew of *Apollo 15* in 1971, when astronauts left a marker establishing the first and only college alumni chapter on the moon.

Above: Alumna Mary Frances Berry, historian and activist, chaired the U.S. Commission on Civil Rights. Image: Jim Abbott

Left: In 1965, alumnus Edward H. White II became the first American to walk in space as part of *Gemini IV*, piloted by fellow U-M James McDivitt. Image: NASA

"She was—officially—Michigan's only Homecoming Queen for Life."

STAR FACULTY
The Force of Doc Losh

By James Tobin

On Football Saturdays for many years, a woman presided at the toss of the coin.

She was no cheerleader, no drum majorette.

She was a short woman of a certain age and generous girth, with graying hair and flowing skirts of the kind seen most often on beloved maiden aunts—though few such aunts wore a Michigan letter sweater.

She was a tenured professor of astronomy, the first woman ever to hold that position at Michigan.

She was the owner of a sideline pass to Michigan Stadium and the pins or lavalieres of 10 Michigan fraternities—possibly more; she lost track of the exact number.

She was the published author of scientific papers and a radio personality who instructed audiences on the mysteries of the night sky.

She was—officially—Michigan's only Homecoming Queen for Life.

She may have been the most popular teacher in the University's history. In a career that stretched from the presidency of Calvin Coolidge to the election of Richard Nixon, the total number of her students apparently exceeded 50,000.

She was known to all—from timid freshmen in the back row of her classroom to long-retired All-Americans at gala dinners on the eve of Rose Bowls—by a stubby name of seven letters: Doc Losh.

In her time, Doc Losh was there at the 50-yard line whenever the Wolverines took the field for a home game. Image: Hazel Marie Losh Collection, Bentley Historical Library

61

On the Rise

Hazel Marie Losh was born in the summer of the Spanish-American War—the summer of 1898—in the village of Blanchester, Ohio. As a girl she loved the stars, and after her graduation from Ohio Wesleyan University, she came to Ann Arbor to seek a master's degree in astronomy.

She expected to become a teacher of high school Latin. But Professor William J. Hussey, director of U-M's Detroit Observatory, saw her promise as a scientist. He designed a program of study for her that would lead to a Ph.D. She took it, earning her doctorate in 1924.

She taught briefly at Smith College, then spent two years at the prestigious Wilson Observatory in California—the first woman with a Ph.D. on that staff.

In 1927 she returned to Ann Arbor, becoming the first female member of the Department of Astronomy. (For a time she was also Hussey's secretary.)

That fall she saw the first football game played in Michigan Stadium—a 33–0 victory against her alma mater, Ohio Wesleyan. It was the start of a love affair.

Moonstruck

In the classroom she became popular for clear, straightforward explanations of the mysteries of the cosmos.

"I guess I'm simple-minded," she once said, "for I've often been accused of being able to make things plain and understandable. But I think if someone, even a so-called 'expert,' can't explain something to you, can't reduce it to a clear and basic level, then perhaps it is they who have a problem, not you."

She was not much interested in the rise of astrophysics, which, in her era in the classroom, was transforming the study of astronomy as she had learned it as a girl.

She said: "There's a great tendency toward some of this highbrow astronomy, space and all, rather than in what I call the old fundamental astronomy, about the phases of the moon and just ordinary facts. You know, it's surprising how many people don't want to teach anything like that. . . .

"Many people think astronomy began only in the last few

years with the ventures into space. I try to show my students that all that has happened in space travel wouldn't have been possible without the discoveries of scientists like Newton and Keppler."

She published esoteric research in her field, but it was her ability in the classroom that built her renown. Her simple eloquence about the heavens can be glimpsed in the manuscript of an undated lecture she gave—before the Apollo space flights—on "The Moon and Eclipses":

> Let us go out into the moonlight. It is a summer night and the Moon is full with its round golden disk hanging low in the southeast. . . . The Moon is so familiar to all of us, and we know so much about it, yet almost half of its surface has never been seen by man, and will ever remain a mystery. The reason that it keeps the same face toward the Earth is because it turns on its axis in exactly the same period that it takes to revolve around the Sun. . . .
>
> What lies on the other side? Is it like the familiar face, or the 'Man in the Moon,' that we see over and over again, or does it conceal surprises such as man has never witnessed? But the Moon will never turn around, and therefore her unseen face will always remain an unsolved riddle to man, the moonstruck and otherwise.

> "I have loved the stars too fondly to be fearful of the night."

"The Best Teacher I Ever Had"

During World War II she corresponded with former students all over the planet. One of them was a young Army sergeant stationed in the South Pacific, R. David Matthews.

He had a problem, Matthews wrote "Miss Losh" in April 1945, two years after taking her course.

"The skies look a lot different from down here than they did in Ann Arbor," he said, and a certain bright star—or was it the planet Venus?—was defying his effort to identify it with a star chart. Could she help?

"I might add that watching the stars has given me many hours of pleasure since I came overseas and many times guard duty at night was made more enjoyable."

Another student, a Coast Guard ensign stationed in the North Atlantic, was thinking of Losh as he wrote to a friend back in Ann Arbor in 1943.

"I took some astronomy in Michigan, never dreaming I

would ever have any use for it," wrote Philip F. Wicklund, "but the little I can remember of it now comes in handy. . . . Do you know Dr. Losh of the Astronomy Dept.? If so, please tell her that the astronomy I learned at Michigan has been of the greatest help to me in the study of celestial navigation."

Her teaching, however old school, stuck with a great many students, including some who went on to distinguished careers in her field.

"Doc Losh," said Kenneth Yoss, an astronomer at the University of Illinois, "was the best teacher I ever had teach me anything."

A for Athletes

Since the 1930s, her introductory course in astronomy had been attracting—among many other students—large numbers of Michigan athletes. She liked them and they liked her, and it came to be said that she graded on the following curve: A for athletes, B for boys, and C for coeds.

Whenever she heard this repeated, she would say: "And D for the dummies who believed it."

Nonetheless, the lists of Michigan stars in her grade books grew longer by the year—then by the decade.

She taught Bennie Oosterbaan. She taught Tom Harmon—"a good student and a great athlete." Ron Kramer cleaned telescopes for her. She taught Bill Freehan. Cazzie Russell took her class in the first term of his freshman year.

She accounted for her long friendship with Michigan athletics like many another fan: There was just "something magical," she said, about Football Saturdays.

"Of course, astronomy is the reason I'm here. And it was my first reason for being here and the thing I've liked from the time I was a child," she said late in her career. "But still, you can't just have astronomy all the time."

She certainly didn't.

Superfan

Records are hazy on precisely when Doc Losh began to play her large public role in the Michigan football program. But the tradition was so revered by the 1970s that when a mix-up prevented her from crossing the field as usual before the game—and Michigan wound up in a tie—the disaster was widely blamed on whoever had failed to get Doc Losh to her appointed post.

By then she had become some combination of superfan and supermascot, a totemic touchstone rather like the Brown Jug and the Mud Bowl—symbols of Michigan's Michigan-ness that could never be replaced by standard-issue Super Bowl theatrics. In the postwar era, as mores changed and students abandoned old traditions, Doc Losh's presence at a game or a pep rally offered a living link to a time when those traditions had mattered deeply. Thanks to her, they somehow mattered still.

At pep rallies she would deliver prophecies and sheer hokum, like this talk on the eve of the Purdue game in 1965, half schoolgirl poetry, half incantation to the pigskin gods:

> We must play this game tomorrow in the true Michigan spirit.
> We must win this game in the true Michigan tradition.
> Tradition—oh, that precious voice, that speaks down through the years
> And whispers to its stalwart sons, when doubt of Victory nears
> It lives in hearts of Michigan men—yes, and it always will
> Our boys believe in Michigan, up there on Stadium Hill.

Hazel "Doc" Losh, the first woman to be a tenured professor of astronomy at Michigan, strikes a pose in the Detroit Observatory. Image: Hazel Marie Losh Collection, Bentley Historical Library

Last Chapter

She never married. "You can call me an old maid if you want to, I don't care," she said late in life. "You know, there's a time when you're younger when being called that kind of bothers you, but at my age, I couldn't care less."

She was a pioneer on behalf of her sex but never thought about it much. "I'm not a suffragette," she said during the feminist surge of the 1970s. "I'm not a women's libber. I never had any difficulties. I most certainly haven't any complaint. But they make more of a fuss about it, certainly, now."

Even so, among her papers she kept this fragment of an old poem attributed to 19th century journalist Kate Field, copied on her manual typewriter on an index card:

> *They talk about a woman's sphere*
> *As though it had a limit*

There's not a place in earth or heaven
There's not a task to mankind given
There's not a blessing or a woe
There's not a whispered yes or no
There's not a life, there's not a birth
That has a feather's weight of worth
Without a woman in it

Even after she stepped down from her active faculty appointment in 1968, she taught for several more years, and from her house on East University she made the three-block walk to her office in the Dennison Building nearly every day. She kept up with the astronomy journals and taped a radio show called "Astronomy Report" that played on public radio stations across the state.

She directed that her tombstone be inscribed with words from "The Old Astronomer to His Pupil," by the 19th-century English poet Sarah Williams: *I have loved the stars too fondly to be fearful of the night.*

Sick with cancer, she missed the home opener in 1978 against Illinois. On Saturday, September 30, she was escorted to the game against Duke by her physician, U-M surgeon Errol E. Erlandson. They watched Michigan trounce the Blue Devils, 52–0. She died a few days later.

"She was," said President Robben Fleming, "an institution within an institution."

THIS IS MICHIGAN

UNIQUE TEACHING. Michigan has consistently transformed the classroom experience, starting with the decision to offer a scientific course in parallel with the traditional classical course (1852), followed by the seminary method of teaching (1871) and offering elective courses (1877). This continued in U-M's second century with a depth of interdisciplinary teaching and research rarely found elsewhere in the academy; U-M has more faculty with joint appointments than anywhere else. The Center for Research on Learning and Teaching is the oldest such program in the country and a model for promoting excellence in college teaching.

A team of U-M paleontologists, led by Daniel Fisher, work to excavate a mammoth's remains from a farmer's field near Ann Arbor in 2015. Image: Daryl Marshke, Michigan Photography

DRIVEN TO PERFECTION

Revelli and Michigan's Bands

By Kim Clarke

*H*e is an old man, with creases at his eyes and
white, thinning hair. He appears particularly
small, even for someone who never stood more
than 5′7″.

*He is in the autumn of his years in 1992. All
eyes are on him as he crosses the Hill Auditorium
stage in a slow but determined walk. Steps on the
podium. Lifts his arms. Readies the baton.*

The world is suddenly young again.

*The unmistakable, joyful noise of a Sousa
march is splendid and bursting with life.
Flutes and clarinets dance above their brassy
counterparts. The snare drum is crisp. The music
races and slows, soars and dips like a roller-coaster
ride.*

*The guest conductor is William Revelli,
legendary leader of the University of Michigan
Bands, a pioneer in American music education,
and a John Philip Sousa acolyte.*

*He is directing "The George Washington
Bicentennial March," the last work of the March
King. It is a personal favorite—difficult to play, but
so worth the effort.*

*In conducting his hero's final composition,
Revelli is making his last appearance at Hill, a
place where he first set foot 56 years ago as a junior
professor who had been handed an anemic college
band.*

Certain names connote leadership, at Michigan
and beyond: Tappan. Angell. Yost. Bo.
Revelli.

Revelli and the marching
band drum section in
1954. Image: William D.
Revelli Papers, Bentley
Historical Library

69

His love of teaching, his belief that music is as sustaining as water and oxygen, and his unrelenting drive for perfection resonate long after his final note.

Michigan's bands grew from one to seven during his tenure. His methods shaped band pedagogy from middle school through college. His faith in students carried them across the country and around the globe, exposing them to different cultures and showcasing the University of Michigan to the world.

Michigan traditions—a high-stepping marching band, pep bands, colorful halftime shows, Band-O-Rama, symphony tours—all have their roots in Revelli.

His demands ("Stop conducting me!"), his exasperation ("Why don't you get a hammer and be done with it?"), and his encouragement ("Be dedicated in whatever you do—even if it's kissing your girl goodnight") ring in alumni ears generations after graduating.

At the core of it all was his credo: "We do not teach music. Rather, we teach people through music."

A Boy and His Violin

It's a pitch-black Sunday morning in 1909 and seven-year-old Willie Revelli is standing along the railroad tracks in the tiny Illinois coal town of Panama. In the distance, a train's whistle sings. Willie snaps on his flashlight, raises his arm, and flags down the massive locomotive.

In his other hand is his precious violin. It is the only instrument he ever wanted, and he wasn't yet five when he began begging for one.

"My dad put it right beside my bed on a stand and when I woke up Christmas morning, there was my violin! The first thing I wanted to do was play; of course all I could do was scratch around."

This is why he waits at the train station. Wake up Sunday mornings at 4:30, hop aboard The Limited, and ride four hours to the big city of St. Louis. There, he meets with the concertmaster of the St. Louis Symphony Orchestra for a 45-minute violin lesson, followed by free time and the return trip to Panama. He arrives home after 9 p.m.

He does this every Sunday, every month, for 10 years.

As a boy not yet 10, Willie Revelli saw John Philip Sousa and

> "What truly mattered to him, though, could not be captured in brick, stone or engraved plaques. It was the ability, and obligation, to inspire."

his band at the Illinois State Fair. He could not believe the sheer majesty of what he was hearing.

"Sousa's band hadn't played two minutes and I knew that's what I wanted to do," he once told an interviewer. "I said, 'Dad, I want to be a conductor like Mr. Sousa.'"

He practiced his violin constantly; he'd rather practice than play outside, unless maybe there was a game of baseball he could join. "I wasn't fooling around just to have music as an avocation but rather to look at it as an experience that would be lifelong."

Panama was a mining town, and he had no intention of spending a lifetime underground, in the dark and danger of the earth. After high school, he moved north and enrolled at the Chicago Musical College (today the Chicago College of Performing Arts at Roosevelt University). Bachelor's degree in hand, William Revelli was about to embark on his career and cultivate his reputation as both bandleader and taskmaster.

Hobart High School

The new music teacher is Mr. Revelli and he barely looks old enough to be out of high school himself.

But here is he, 23 years old in 1925, huddled in the chemistry lab of Indiana's tiny Hobart High School, with a handful of anxious students who want to be in a band.

None of them has ever touched a musical instrument.

Concert and marching bands—staples of today's K-12 system and colleges—were an American phenomenon in the 1920s. In the wake of the Great War, the public embraced patriotism and pomp, along with music spread by the phonograph. A growing middle class preferred band music rather than fussier orchestras.

The school band movement was under way.

At Hobart, Revelli's official duties called for him to teach vocal music, as well as conduct several school choirs and a glee club. He also received permission to develop a band program.

The students honked and squeaked and generally crashed through the music. There were not enough players to form a full concert band, and they performed minus several standard instruments. He called it "mess production."

Revelli and his violin, circa 1924. Image: William D. Revelli Papers, Bentley Historical Library

Still, Hobart parents were keen to hear their young prodigies.

"I had mothers calling and asking me when their child was going to bring his or her instrument home. I used to say, 'You know, Mrs. Maybaum, you don't know how lucky you are. I have to listen to him, you don't. You should be thankful.'"

He demanded, and expected, excellence. During one frustrating practice, he threw down his baton and told the students to just go home. He wouldn't conduct them if they were the last band on earth. He stormed out of the room.

Stunned, the students did not move. Ten minutes passed before Revelli returned and resumed the rehearsal.

He could not deny how much they energized him. "Anytime I was down, all I had to do was give a lesson, and those kids pulled me right out of it."

In return, they played their hearts out. The Hobart High School band matured and for five straight years, reigned as finest in the country. Revelli's reputation grew; professional symphonies, colleges and bigger high schools pursued him. "I wanted to make one move and I wanted it to be the right one."

That right one was Michigan.

The Marching Band

He is in full band regalia. White gloves, jacket, epaulets and a navy blue cap with the distinctive block "M."

Before him sit dozens of freshmen, sheer brawn and muscle, the newest members of the Michigan football team. Coach Bo Schembechler is in his debut season, and the veteran band director has offered to help the team in any way he can.

Teach my players the fight song, Schembechler asked.

The director steps up and stares hard at the athletes.

"JOHN PHILIP SOUSA CALLED THIS THE GREATEST FIGHT SONG EVER WRITTEN. AND YOU WILL SING IT WITH RESPECT."

Sing they do. Out of their chairs, standing and booming, "Hail! To the victors valiant. Hail! To the conquering heroes. Hail! Hail!"

Revelli is invited back every season.

"God," Schembechler will say years later, "he was beautiful."

In a way, William Revelli steps onto the field every time today's Michigan Marching Band pours out of the Michigan Stadium tunnel.

In his 36 years, Revelli revolutionized not only the Michigan style, but marching bands across the nation. He dropped the name "Michigan Fighting One Hundred" ("It didn't have any class to it") and launched the "Michigan Marching Band." He quickened the stride of players, who now took more steps to cover the same amount of yardage. Where the U.S. Army band took 120 steps a minute, the Michigan Marching Band packed in 176.

And he ranted.

"I don't want it just about right! To me, just about right is terrible!"

"Mister, if you can't play that, what CAN you play?"

"It's all the fault of your high school band director."

He and his assistants introduced thematic halftime shows, abandoning performances that mimicked military drills. The band took the shape of a Thanksgiving turkey, or a car with spinning wheels traversing the field. ("I know it's hard—that's what makes it difficult!")

Perhaps his most significant contribution was the sound of the band itself. He wanted his marching band to sound like a symphonic band that just happened to be on a football field.

Thousands of high school band students would converge on Michigan Stadium for the annual Band Day instituted by Revelli, shown conducting in 1959. Image: William D. Revelli Papers, Bentley Historical Library

"Don't come up and tell me the Michigan band looked good; I don't like that kind of compliment. But it you say they looked great and they sounded terrific, I'll accept that compliment."

That meant exceptional tone. "Even if it was November and snow was coming down, I stopped that band if there was a bad sound. I did it a million times. I didn't care if the game was the next day. What I did care about was their sound—right now! I want a good tone!"

The Symphony Band

It is the opening concert of an international tour that will cover 30,000 miles, 110 performances and 21 cities. Tonight they play for Moscow, a city that in 1961 has rare contact with Americans, their universities or their young people.

The Michigan students have put on an exceptional performance for nearly two hours, and are concluding with a Russian classic, Mussorgsky's majestic "Great Gate of Kiev." Revelli braces for the applause he knows will explode after this grand finale.

Instead there is silence.

Frozen, he stares at his students. It seems as if all oxygen has left the hall.

After a moment that spans forever, a single Russian rises. He claps, once, and the audience of 6,000 mimics him. Then they clap again, slowly, and again, faster and faster again, now they are stamping their feet, and clapping and stamping, thousands of hands and feet pounding away.

The Symphony Band plays five encores.

If you wanted to get under Bill Revelli's skin, you called him the director of the Michigan Marching Band.

"Not because I am not proud to be director of the marching band; of course I am. But wouldn't you believe that after a half a century they would know that I am director of all University bands?"

The Symphony Band was the finest of the bands he came to create and conduct. It was the cream, rich with music majors and aspiring professionals. Where concert bands were traditionally identified as brassy and harsh, Revelli's symphony band had a silky elegance to it; his clarinets could sound like violins, the euphoniums like cellos.

The Michigan Symphony Band performs at the Moscow Sports Palace in February 1961. Image: William D. Revelli Papers, Bentley Historical Library

They would practice, practice and practice some more. Start a piece. Stop. Start over. Stop. Start again. Stop. Over and over, until it was right.

He began taking the Symphony Band on the road—a first for a major university—and they performed in America's great venues. The pinnacle was the 1961 tour, a goodwill gesture arranged by the U.S. State Department as the Cold War burned. The Michigan band would tour for 15 weeks and visit nine countries, including two months in the Soviet Union. It remains the most extensive tour ever carried out by a university band.

The tour concluded at Carnegie Hall and the praise was lavish.

"The Michigan ensemble . . . played with the precision of a well-oiled machine," wrote Raymond Ericson in the *New York Times*. "More than that, it produced some luscious, gleaming organ-like sonorities within performances that were always accurate, texturally clean, and smooth flowing."

This was Revelli perfection.

Revelli was guest conductor for Keith Brion and the New Sousa Band during a 1992 performance at Hill Auditorium. Image: University Musical Society

Coda

It's halftime and more than 106,000 fans are jammed into Michigan Stadium for 1992's homecoming.

The marching band is on the field and at attention, as are dozens of alumni players who have returned for this fall ritual. They eye the 90-year-old conductor, retired for more than 20 years, and wait for his cue.

"God Bless America" soars from their instruments. He commands the field, and then turns to face the stands. Again he conducts. Together, with the Michigan faithful, they sing in unison.

The applause begins well before the final note.

He was Mr. Revelli, Dr. Revelli or the Chief. He was charming and he was a tyrant. He worked incredible hours and he never grew tired.

"Do you know how many times I've conducted 'The Victors'? Thousands! Do I ever conduct it like I'm bored with it? I don't care if I conduct it for a hundred years, every time I conduct it, I have never conducted it the time I'm going to conduct it. That makes it a premiere performance."

Revelli died in 1994. He founded the College Band Directors National Association and was inducted into both the Music Educators Hall of Fame and the Hall of Fame of Distinguished Band Conductors. The marching band facility at Michigan bears his name.

What truly mattered to him, though, could not be captured in brick, stone or engraved plaques. It was the ability, and obligation, to inspire.

"You are not a conductor of bands, you're a conductor of people. It's through music that you reach them, and it's a beautiful way to reach people."

THIS IS MICHIGAN

ACOUSTIC PERFECTION. Hill Auditorium is an acoustically superb performance hall that has attracted the likes of Enrico Caruso, Ravi Shankar, Jessye Norman and Bruce Springsteen. Leonard Bernstein called it one of his three favorite concert halls. It has embodied the University's role as a forum for debate and ideas by hosting such speakers as William Howard Taft, Eleanor Roosevelt, Angela Davis, Hillary Clinton and Desmond Tutu.

Two classics: The New York Philharmonic performs the film score of *On the Waterfront* in 2015. Image: Austin Thomason, Michigan Photography

U. S. NAVAL TRAINING SCHOOL (W. R.)
THE BRONX, NEW YORK, N. Y.

Dear Aunt Ruth....

What is that old phrase about "warming the cockles of one'
heart?" Anyway, that's what your sweet letter did for me
today....I had no idea of your hugh correspondence, and be
me when I say that <u>my</u> note meant more to me than I can tel
And I'm so thrilled to be your first Wave! Surely, though
any of the others knew of you, you've most probably be swa

As a matter of fact, I got your name through a friend of m
a Lt. Bob Barrie of the Naval Air Corps. Bob and I have b
great friends since our sophmore year...way back there in

---

75 **Company "C" 291st I**
Seventy-Fifth Division

Dear Aunt Ruth,

I have really enjoyed rea
bundles of Dailies that you s
Especially of interest has be
of the May Festival and t
of next year's Choral Union
read this letter, how I
all the more! When I
I imagine you

U. S. S. PADUCAH
c/o Postmaster
New York, N. J.
February 22, 1942

Dear Aunt Ruth—

I'm sorry that I haven't
able to answer your letters and
sooner, but I hope you will un
stand that our time isn't exa
our own these days and that i
was an oversight.

Your letters were sure swel
made me feel as though I h
really an Aunt in Ann Arbo
Valentine card was very nice.
ha been thinking of you often, but
it
get

345th BOMBARDMENT GROU

AIR APACHES

June 13, 1945
Luzon, Philippi

Dear Aunt Ruth,

I do hope you
long delay in wri
forwarded you lette
ago and I just rece
day. I have moved
coming overseas so

Dear Mrs. Buchanan;

The great adventure f
is about to **begin**. We are
New York--awaiting further

_____ This post

_____ It is constantly di
hush. This letter will
know how much of the descr
It has rained and snowed si
the soldiers to look forwar
This will be _____
is nothing if not somber I
almost as eagerly as does a
enlightening and I suppose
this trip ad nauseam. Good
a happy one. **OVER**

UNITED STATES ARMY

Sept. 10, 1944

Dear Aunt Ruth,

Here I am back in camp and all settled down
again. I've been back almost two weeks. I had a swell
time on my furlough and was very glad I had a chance
to visit you while I was in Ann Arbor. While home
I went swimming, bowling, roller skating, dancing, bicycling
and even on a boat ride to Bob-Lo. I sure wish it
could have been longer.

"DEAR AUNT RUTH"

By Kim Clarke

Ruth Bacon Buchanan at her desk on campus. Image: Ruth Bacon Buchanan Papers, Bentley Historical Library

Night after night during World War II, Ruth Buchanan would leave her workplace at the University of Michigan and return home to her second job.

By the thousands and with clockwork precision, Buchanan wrote to U-M students, faculty, staff and alumni serving in the war. She mailed letters, greeting cards, and copies of the *Michigan Daily.* Whether they were stationed stateside, recuperating in hospitals, or seeing action in Europe and the Pacific, students could expect to hear news about Ann Arbor from Buchanan.

Her correspondence was staggering: 17,828 letters; 6,952 birthday cards; 7,398 get-well cards. Over the course of the war, she mailed more than 57,000 copies of the *Daily* to servicemen and servicewomen with U-M ties.

"When the war started I wanted to help," Buchanan told an Ann Arbor radio station. "It was hard to find how I could, though. I'm down here at the Museum six and a half days a week. . . . I decided to write to maybe 25 boys. In the end it was almost 2,200."

Their responses, archived at the Bentley Historical Library, are a window into the mindset of students encountering all aspects of war: camaraderie, loss, boredom, culture clash, and a deep longing for home. In particular, students' reminiscences of U-M carry themes that resonate with generations of alumni.

"The other Saturday I heard a snatch of the Michigan game over the radio, but it didn't last

Letters received by Ruth Bacon Buchanan during World War II. Images: Ruth Bacon Buchanan Papers, Bentley Historical Library

James R. Terrell, right, a 1943 Michigan graduate, was a frequent correspondent. Image: Ruth Bacon Buchanan Papers, Bentley Historical Library

Buchanan's tally of her massive wartime correspondence. Ruth Bacon Buchanan Papers, Bentley Historical Library

clipping.....10528
    Total.. 67384

to whom I have been writing......1217
omen 1013
                        Total..2230

my "war record"—
    Ruth Bacon Buchanan—
        aunt Ruth to men
        and women in service

long enough to learn the score. However, it took me back to the old days and, in fact, made me rather homesick," wrote Philip F. Wicklund, who graduated in 1938 and served in the Coast Guard. ("Little did I dream when I left the stately portals of Angell Hall that in four years I would be running around in bell-bottom pants. But so it goes.")

Regardless of the letterhead or return address, students' letters carry a consistent salutation: "Dear Aunt Ruth." Divorced with three adult stepsons, all of whom earned U-M degrees, Buchanan saw the students as nieces and nephews and requested they call her Aunt Ruth. They obliged by the thousands.

Buchanan was an unassuming but dedicated receptionist at the Exhibit Museum, and most student-soldiers had no idea who she was when her letters arrived. But they were grateful that someone from Ann Arbor was reaching out to them, and in return they showered Buchanan with mail.

"I know somewhat how you feel now when the postman brings you in a batch of letters," wrote Richard C. Emery, a 1943 Engineering graduate and Navy officer. "I got 26 all in one sitting the other day, and it certainly made a marvelous day out of an otherwise dull one."

Students' affection for Buchanan is abundant in their letters. They invited her to their weddings, and shared news of promotions, honors and broken hearts. Several sent small souvenirs—military patches, postcards, foreign currency and photographs. Others mailed dollar bills to help with paper and postage costs. Still others said they heard from Buchanan more than from their own families.

"You know, Aunt Ruth, since I have been in the Navy I've learned so much about life in such a short while. You'd be surprised really," wrote Navy Lt. (j.g.) Arlie Reagan, who graduated in 1943 and served in the Pacific Theater. "My life has taken on so much added meaning that it astounds me. I've begun to realize 'just what the score is.' What liberty, freedom, the pursuit of happiness that I've heard so much about really means. People, I believe, just don't realize how serious this thing really is. I certainly didn't until I came face to face with realities here and about."

THIS IS MICHIGAN

ATOMIC GIANTS. The Summer Symposia in Physics in the 1920s and 1930s brought the world's greatest physicists to Ann Arbor. Such figures as Hans Bethe, Wolfgang Pauli and Enrico Fermi met to exchange findings and teach small seminars on theoretical physics, the branch of science that transformed our understanding of the universe and led, with profound consequences, to the development of atomic weapons and energy.

Enrico Fermi, in suit, on campus in 1928 for the summer physics sessions. Physics Professor George Uhlenbeck is at the far left. Image: Samuel Goudsmit Collection, Emilio Segre Visual Archives, American Institute of Physics

A QUIET PIONEER
Medicine's Elizabeth Crosby

By Whitley Hill

In the 1890s, as she played in the fields and forests around her log home in Petersburg—a small farm town in southeastern Michigan—the world must have seemed a fascinating place to a tiny, brilliant girl named Elizabeth Caroline Crosby.

Life abounded everywhere: turtles and fish; cats and dogs and farm animals; neighbors and classmates with their eccentricities and singular patterns of behavior. Crosby's long career as a comparative neuroanatomist began in those fields and took her to laboratories, classrooms and lecterns around the world. In her remarkable 64-year association with the U-M Medical School, she laid the foundation for today's neuroscience and is estimated to have taught, and inspired, more than 8,000 medical students.

Elizabeth Crosby at age 20. Image: Elizabeth Caroline Crosby Papers, Bentley Historical Library

"A Little Country Girl"

Crosby was born in 1888. She learned to read before she learned to walk. In school, she discovered she loved math and puzzles.

In 1907, she entered nearby Adrian College. Within three years, she had completed a teaching degree and fallen in love with science. She decided to seek out C. Judson Herrick, a well-known neuroanatomist at the University of Chicago.

Opposite page: Elizabeth Crosby in the classroom. Image: Elizabeth Caroline Crosby Papers, Bentley Historical Library

"I was a very scared and not too well-prepared little country girl who had never seen an elevated train," Crosby recalled years later. She went directly to Herrick's office and told him that she'd come all the way from Adrian College to study biology with him. Though he felt she was unprepared, Herrick was swayed by her confidence. He allowed her to work in the dissecting room with the medical students and gave her permission to attend his medical course in neuroanatomy. Within weeks, she was working at the level of medical students with far more formal preparation.

In neuroanatomy ("the great and glorious sweep of the evolution of the brain from the lowest to the highest vertebrates," as she once put it), Crosby found her life's work. She earned a master of science degree in 1912, took a fellowship in anatomy, and graduated magna cum laude with a Ph.D. in 1915, all at the University of Chicago. Her thesis, "The Forebrain of Alligator mississippiensis," published in the *Journal of Comparative Neurology* in 1917, was considered a major contribution to her field.

Crosby's next step was to return home to Petersburg—her parents were in poor health—and take a job as principal of the high school. She taught Latin, zoology, math and English, and even coached the boys' basketball team. She continued her research in the family garage, where she kept young alligators in a washtub. But Crosby was desperate to return to a proper academic setting.

Life at Michigan

In 1920, she walked into Michigan's Department of Anatomy and asked if she might be granted a corner in which to work. Dr. G. Carl Huber, director of the anatomical laboratories, knew of Crosby and hired her as a junior instructor in the anatomy and histology labs. The two fell into an easy research partnership and went on to publish six papers about reptile brains and the optic tectum in reptiles and birds.

Crosby was a master teacher from her very first class at Michigan. Although she prepared copious notes, she never referred to them. Kind, clear and patient, she was loved by her students and she loved them back.

Crosby worked long hours, often seven days a week, and lived simply in a series of rented rooms. But her work and her increasing renown opened the world to her. She made regular

Lecturing in 1959. Image: Elizabeth Caroline
Crosby Papers, Bentley Historical Library

trips to Europe for further study. In 1925, C.U. Ariëns Kappers, head of the Institute for Brain Research in Amsterdam, asked Crosby and Huber to translate and revise his seminal work, *The Comparative Anatomy of the Nervous System of Vertebrates, Including Man,* a task that took 10 years. The resulting volume was so detailed that some say it effectively marked the end of the descriptive phase of neuroanatomy.

But this achievement also marked the beginning of Crosby's most turbulent years at Michigan. In 1934, Huber died. Without her mentor and collaborator, Crosby began to doubt her value to the Medical School. At the same time, other institutions were actively recruiting her. Over the next few years, she resigned at least five times—and each time was convinced to stay.

Crosby continued to weigh other options, however. By now she was a full professor in the Medical School—the first woman to achieve that rank. In 1939, in a move grudgingly

Elizabeth Crosby. Image: Elizabeth Caroline Crosby Papers, Bentley Historical Library

approved by the Medical School, she traveled to Scotland's University of Aberdeen to organize the first courses in histology and neuroanatomy there.

When she returned to Michigan in 1940, she brought with her something completely unexpected: a daughter.

Mother, Partner, Medalist

There are several versions of how, in her early 50s, Elizabeth Crosby—world-renowned neuroanatomist, unmarried and having little experience with children—became the mother of Kathleen Rosena Robb, a vivacious 14-year-old Scot with red curls.

One account is that the girl's father, an impoverished gardener in Aberdeen, begged Crosby to take his youngest daughter far from the dangers of World War II. Another is that Crosby became friends with the Robb family and connected deeply with the child. Still another is that Kathleen climbed a tree in her backyard, which adjoined Crosby's, and fell over an old stone wall and into Crosby's life.

Adopting Kathleen—and taking on the care and education of a young Detroit girl, Suzanne McCotter, a few years later—demonstrated a level of compassion tucked behind the façade of a tiny, studious, middle-aged spinster.

Crosby shared the later years of her life with Dr. Tryphena Humphrey, whom she called "Trap." Originally a protégé of Crosby, who oversaw her U-M dissertation, Humphrey went on to a 28-year collaboration with Dr. Davenport Hooker at the University of Pittsburgh, studying physiological neuroembryology. Humphrey and Crosby shared a home on and off, traveled together frequently and co-authored papers.

The sheer volume of Crosby's published work, and the awards, accolades and lectures, attest to an almost impossibly productive career. And she was an extraordinary teacher of neuroanatomy. On the last day of each course, students sprang to their feet, applauding, and presented her with a bouquet of roses, her favorite flower. In 1957, the Galens Medical Society established the Elizabeth C. Crosby Award for outstanding teaching in the basic sciences.

Crosby's retirement in 1958 did not slow her pace; in fact, it marked the beginning of a second career in which she applied her encyclopedic knowledge of the nervous system to neuro-

Elizabeth Crosby receives the National Medal of Science from President Jimmy Carter in 1980. Image: Elizabeth Caroline Crosby Papers, Bentley Historical Library

surgery. She worked alongside Dr. Edgar Kahn, Dr. Richard C. Schneider, and others in the Department of Neurosurgery, often accompanying them into the operating room to consult on difficult cases.

In 1963, at the age of 75, Crosby joined the faculty of the University of Alabama, in Birmingham, where Humphrey was teaching. And for the next 18 years, Crosby commuted, by plane, back to Ann Arbor for two weeks at a time, staying in a room at the Michigan League, continuing her work. She suffered from osteoporosis and often used crutches—and was known to wave one, in good humor, at anyone who tried to assist her.

Tryphena Humphrey died in 1971. In 1980, Crosby traveled to Washington, D.C., to receive the National Medal of Science from President Jimmy Carter; she made the president hold her crutches as a photographer snapped pictures.

Crosby returned to Michigan in 1981 and eventually moved into daughter Kathleen's home in Dexter. Her son-in-law drove her to the lab every day. On July 28, 1983, at the age of 94, Crosby died at home with Kathleen at her side. On her chest was a paper she'd been working on; in her hand was a pen.

THIS IS MICHIGAN

MEDICAL MIRACLES. Michigan's contributions to medicine and public health have saved lives and enriched communities. Alumna Dr. Alice Hamilton pioneered the study of occupational health and is credited with improving workplace safety. Dr. Aldred Warthin was one of the first medical scientists to make a persuasive case that cancer was heritable in humans. Dr. James Neel unlocked the genetic cause of sickle-cell anemia, and geneticist Dr. Francis Collins discovered the genes for cystic fibrosis and neurofibromatosis ("Elephant Man's disease"). Surgeon William Bartlett developed the extracorporeal membrane oxygenation technology known as ECMO that continues to save thousands of lives.

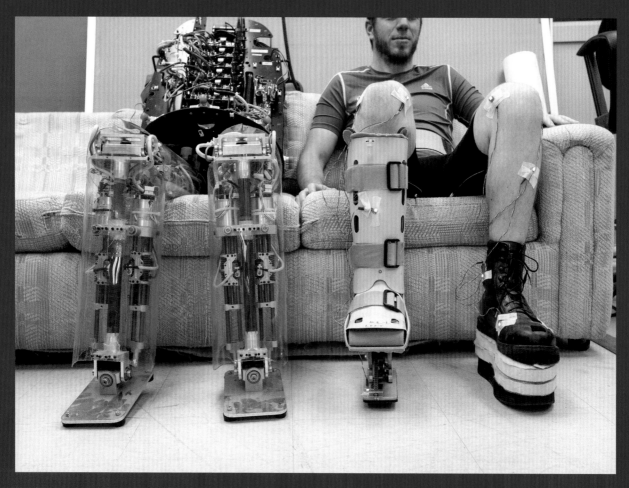

Testing out a prosthetic foot in the Human Biomechanics and Control Lab in 2014. Image: Austin Thomason, Michigan Photography

THIS IS MICHIGAN

ADVANCING VACCINES. Under the direction of Dr. Thomas Francis, U-M conducted extensive clinical trials in 1954 that confirmed the effectiveness of the Salk polio vaccine. The discovery helped to end one of the major medical scourges of the 20th century. Francis and Dr. Jonas Salk had earlier developed the influenza vaccine that protected American soldiers during World War II. Fifty years after the polio trials, Dr. Hunein Maasab, a student mentored by Francis, developed the first nasal spray flu vaccine, FluMist.

Children participating in U-M's 1954 nationwide field trials of Jonas Salk's polio vaccine. Image: Alumni Association records, Bentley Historical Library

FIRST IN CLASS

Orval Johnson's Biggest Race

By Kim Clarke

He was a black student at a largely white university. A young man in a town where many boardinghouses and shops turned away African-Americans. A quiet athlete, accustomed to racing the clock, challenging a football star cheered by thousands as the most decorated player in campus history.

This had never happened at the University of Michigan.

On paper, Val Johnson didn't stand a chance. But things weren't that black and white for the students of 1948.

Candidates

Two men wanted to be president of the Literature, Science, and Arts Class of 1949: Pete Elliott and Val Johnson.

Peter R. Elliott was the prototypical big man on campus. On the football team, he alternated between quarterback and defensive halfback on a squad that went undefeated for two seasons and won back-to-back national championships. During a 1948 trip to the Rose Bowl, he golfed with Bing Crosby. He would leave Michigan with 12 varsity letters—in football, basketball and golf—an accomplishment never to be repeated.

Handsome, fair-haired and clean cut, Elliott played football alongside his older brother

he Senior Class of the University of Michi-dues and is entitled to discount in certain

Orval W. Johnson

Senior Class President

Johnson's signature on Virginia Stewart Nicklas' senior class membership card. Image: Virginia Stewart Nicklas scrapbooks, Bentley Historical Library

African-American students were all but invisible on campus, shown here in 1947, during Val Johnson's years as a student. Image: William E. Wise Collection, Bentley Historical Library

Chalmers, who was known as "Bump" and, like Pete, an All-American.

Orval Wardel Johnson also was an athlete, but he excelled in track, and track did not generate big crowds or huge headlines. He ran the 100-yard dash in 10 seconds and the 220 in 21.6 seconds; a U-M media guide described him as "the speedy Detroit colored boy," a graduate of Northwestern High School. His 5-foot, 11-inch frame often was immaculately dressed. A four-year letterman, he also was active in the Student Legislature, the Sphinx junior honor society and his East Quad dorm council.

If he stood out, it was because Johnson was exceedingly nice, dubbed "the gentlemanly runner" by coaches and reporters. "If I could make Val mad for a few races," his coach, Ken Doherty, remarked, "he could become world champion."

For now, Johnson would settle for class president. That is, if he could get past the biggest name on campus—and perceptions.

Climate

In photo after yearbook photo, Val Johnson is the lone black face in student groups: Student Legislature, the "M" Club of varsity lettermen, Senior Board, a gathering of class presidents from Education, Pharmacy, Nursing and other schools.

African-American students were all but invisible at Michigan in the 1940s, despite blacks having attended since 1853. When Johnson entered his senior year in the fall of 1948, the campus was booming with more than 20,000 students, a record level driven by more than 10,000 veterans who survived World War II and now crowded U-M classrooms. It is estimated that fewer than 100 students were black—half of 1 percent of the campus.

At the start of the decade, graduate student William H. Boone published a master's thesis about life for black students like him on a nearly all-white campus. His findings were bleak. Black students said they found it harder to pay for school because they were limited to menial part-time jobs, while white students were paid more for better jobs such as store clerks and library assistants. They hesitated to speak up in class for fear of standing out ("I believe I am 'on the spot' and too conspicuous, for everyone turns around and stares when

Val Johnson winning the 440-yard race in a 1948 competition at Yost Fieldhouse. Image: William E. Wise Collection, Bentley Historical Library

I say anything," one reported). And the anxiety of being black in a white world left students feeling stigmatized and mentally wrought by "the undesirable realities of life."

The situation was not much better as the decade drew to a close. Roger W. Wilkins, a black student from Grand Rapids who enrolled in the fall of 1949, found that he and the few classmates who looked like him "were peripheral to campus life."

"I would soon learn that though we could eat in the cafeteria, we could not get our hair cut at the Michigan Union, that 90 percent of the private rooms for rent to students were unavailable to us, that we could not eat (or when we became 21, drink) at the legendary Michigan watering hole, The Pretzel Bell," he wrote years later, "and that the girl friends whom we had yet to meet could not try on clothes as the white girls could at the State Street shops."

Wilkins spent seven years at Michigan, earning bachelor's and law degrees in classes taught entirely by white men. "I was never assigned a book, an essay, a play, a short story, or a poem that was written by a black writer or that suggested that any black person had ever done or thought anything worthwhile in the entire history of the world," he said.

This was Val Johnson's world.

Campaign

The job of class president involved rallying the seniors, building school spirit, coordinating events and activities, and finding ways to give back to the University with a class gift and reunions after graduation. It did not carry political power—that was left to the Student Legislature, to which Johnson had been elected earlier that spring.

When campaigning began in late November of 1948, Johnson supporters—white and black—wandered the dorms handing out buttons and lollipops that urged "Val Johnson for Senior President." At the same time, phones rang throughout the residence halls. Over and over, some 1,200 times, campaign workers played taped messages of a poem that encouraged a vote for Johnson.

Johnson himself visited the dorms, mingling with students and asking for their support.

Turnout was heavy across campus in the 1948 elections. Image: *Michigan Daily*

When election day arrived, the campus woke to biting winds and a rare front-page editorial in the *Michigan Daily,* whose senior editors urged students to head to the polls.

There was other big news in that day's paper. Led by All-American Pete Elliott, the undefeated Michigan football team had finished No. 1 in the season's final Associated Press poll. More than half a million fans had turned out that fall to watch Elliott and his teammates crush their opponents by scores like 35–0, 54–0 and 40–0.

Voting stations were set up across campus, from the Diag and Engineering Arch to the steps of the Law School and lobby of the Michigan Union. Students were casting ballots for dozens of candidates eager to join the Student Legislature, J-Hop Committee, Board in Control of Student Publications, and class officer positions.

Voting would last two days, from 8 a.m. to 5 p.m. Election organizers hoped to store ballots overnight in the city jail, but instead settled for the basement of President Alexander Ruthven's house. After the first day of voting, the *Daily* carried a front-page photo of senior class candidates huddled around a table, presumably discussing their campaigns; Johnson was front and center, and Elliott was absent.

Thousands of students, the *Daily* reported, had turned out at the polls.

Concerns

Despite the dearth of African-Americans on campus—or perhaps, because of it—Michigan students of the late 1940s were agitating for change. They wanted greater racial integration at a time when President Harry Truman ordered the end of segregation in the military and Jackie Robinson broke the color barrier in major league baseball.

The number of student organizations ballooned, with newly created groups such as the Committee for Civil Rights, the Committee to End Discrimination, and the Democratic Socialist Club winning approval from campus administrators. Students formed the Inter-Racial Association, "to work for a purer democracy by combating prejudice and discrimination against race, religion or national origin in the United States and particularly in the Ann Arbor and University area."

Called the IRA, the group was known for hosting popular films on campus and sandwiching in educational shorts about tolerance; when students would settle in for a showing of Alfred Hitchcock's *The 39 Steps,* they first saw a documentary refuting the concept of racial superiority.

IRA members reached out to university officials nationwide to gauge racial issues on campuses and learn how they were being addressed. When the dean of students at the University of Illinois received the IRA's query, he told U-M Dean of Students Joseph Bursley he had no intention of responding—a decision Bursley endorsed.

"I realize fully the tough row which many negros (*sic*) have to hoe and I am glad at any time to do what I can to help them," Bursley wrote in 1946. "Personally I have no objection to sitting next to a negro at a movie or any public place, nor do I object to sitting at the table with him simply because he is negro. I have eaten more than once with colored people and would do so again.

"However, I have no sympathy with the radical trouble makers who are trying to stir up discord and bring about a clash between the whites and colored members of our community."

Students felt otherwise. The IRA carried out Operation Haircut, a boycott of the dozens of Ann Arbor barbershops and beauty parlors that refused to serve black customers. A group of campus veterans lobbied student government to investigate why there were no black students on the varsity basketball and baseball teams. The Student Legislature called upon faculty to teach a course in the psychology of prejudice, another course in black history, and to make prejudice the theme of an English class. Whenever efforts failed, which was often, students took pride in at least having raised awareness of discrimination.

At the same time, graduate students at Michigan were conducting more research about African-Americans than at any predominantly white university in the country. Fifteen studies were under way by U-M master's and doctoral students in 1948, compared with places like Yale University and the University of Chicago, with one study apiece, or Harvard University, which reported no such research.

And in the days leading up to the 1948 elections, the *Daily* made a point of constantly hammering Phi Kappa Psi fraternity for supporting its national organization's policy of refusing black members. The national leaders had just revoked the charter of a Phi Psi chapter at Amherst College for admitting an African-American, and Michigan fraternity members called it the right decision; U-M's Greek system had white and black fraternities, they argued, and the system worked just fine.

The *Daily* wasn't buying it.

"This sounds like the beginning of the argument expressed by the white supremacists of the South," the paper editorialized. "It rationalizes that because there are equal facilities for the different groups, no effort should be made to make them one united body."

Counting

When it came time to tally the votes, in a room at the Union made hazy by cigarette smoke, there were a staggering number of ballots. More than 7,000 students—one-third of the campus—had cast a ballot, with roughly a thousand voting in the Johnson-Elliott race. There had never been such a turnout by students at Michigan.

It was a blowout.

After 10 hours of counting ballots, the outcome was overwhelming and undeniable. By a 2-to-1 margin, Val Johnson trounced Pete Elliott. Seniors had elected their first black class

Seniors Orval Johnson (*above*) and Pete Elliott. Images: William E. Wise Collection, Bentley Historical Library

president, a first not only for Michigan but also for any predominantly white university in the country.

Johnson was running down a stairwell in the Michigan Union when someone told him the outcome. It was 3 o'clock in the morning, the day after polls closed. Behind him, a cheer went up from a Union hallway as other students heard the final results.

"I'm completely overwhelmed," Johnson told a *Daily* reporter.

Days after the votes were tallied, Johnson reflected on his race, his victory, and what both meant for racial relations on campus. "I think it's really a matter of getting acquainted with the different races. I've always believed association and acquaintance were the real solutions to the problem."

He knew he was different, but not because of his skin color. "There's an advantage to standing out as an individual, because if you're liked, you'll probably be remembered."

"The gentlemanly runner" then composed a thank-you note to his classmates, "for the unceasing moral and physical support you accorded me in the recent Senior Presidential campaign."

Conclusion

Val Johnson, Pete Elliott and the Class of 1949 graduated in early June, before thousands of family members and friends gathered at Ferry Field.

Elliott, who earned a degree in history, chose coaching as a career and led college teams at Nebraska, California, Illinois and Miami. He was elected to the College Football Hall of Fame and served as executive director of the Pro Football Hall of Fame for 17 years. He died in 2013 at age 86.

Johnson left to work for United Nations Radio in Paris. Fluent in French and Spanish and with a degree in Latin American studies, he also taught language and communication at the National Autonomous University of Mexico. He then returned to his hometown Detroit to teach high school Spanish. When he died in 1995, he was 69.

THIS IS MICHIGAN

FORGING COMMUNITY. Michigan continually pushes itself to broaden its diversity and strengthen its tolerance, while also acknowledging that its record has blemishes. From the start, teaching and research have been intentionally devoid of religious affiliation. International students have been welcomed since the first decade of classes being offered. Women were admitted in 1870, yet also faced discrimination and double standards for the next century. Campus protests such as the Black Action Movement of the 1970s and #bbum (Being Black at the University of Michigan) revealed inequities in the treatment of African-Americans. At the same time, the University successfully fought before the U.S. Supreme Court in 2003 for the right to use affirmative action in admissions decisions. And U-M was the first university in the country to establish an office to serve gays and lesbians when the Human Sexuality Office (today's Spectrum Center) opened in 1971; 22 years later, U-M banned discrimination based on sexual orientation.

Supporters of affirmative action march across campus on Martin Luther King Day in 2007. Image: Lin Jones, Michigan Photography

REMEMBERING BO

By John U. Bacon

Everyone knew the public Bo: the man on the sidelines berating referees, screaming at players, and smashing his headset against the Astroturf. All true, of course. But the public Bo Schembechler had little to do with the Bo I came to know—the same one his family, friends and former players loved so much.

I first met Bo in 1974, when I was a 10 year old attending a Michigan hockey game. In the second period the p.a. announcer paged Bo Schembechler to meet someone under the north stands. My buddy and I figured, How many Bo Schembechlers can there be?

Sure enough, there he was, chatting up some old friends, while we waited nearby, nervously rolling up our programs. When he saw us standing there, he interrupted his conversation to bellow, "Now what can I do for you, young men?" He signed our programs with care and thanked us for supporting the Wolverines.

They say your character is what you do when you think no one is watching. I've seen Bo pass that test a thousand times, but none was more important to me than that first encounter. If he had ignored me then, I wouldn't be writing this now.

Contrary to his "football-mad" reputation, Schembechler was interested in just about everything—from the Ann Arbor bus system to race-horse breeding to teacher training—and he had an opinion about all of it, too. One semester he audited a class on politics at the Ford School of Public Policy, where he would often admonish his younger classmates to take their hats off.

Bo was a voracious reader, with a weakness for Tom Clancy books. He also loved music,

Bo Schembechler posed in front of football team in 1986. Image: University of Michigan News and Information Service, Bentley Historical Library

101

from Cole Porter to Tina Turner. He hummed constantly. It resonated in his chest, occasionally bubbling up to form a verse, which he sang in a deep baritone—"With YOU, I've gone from RAGS to RICHES. I feel like a MILL-ion-AIRE"—then he'd return to humming while filing some papers.

Above all, Bo was interested in people. When he was in town he'd drive to Schembechler Hall around 10 a.m., park in "Reserved Space 01," and trundle down the second-floor hallway to his office. Schembechler might have been a great coach, but he would have made a terrible spy, with a complete inability to whisper, sneak up on anyone or speak anyone's name in lowercase letters. "Hey MARY!" he would roar at the far end of the hallway, "Howya doin'? Hey, BIG JOHN FALK! What's the good word?!"

Before he could sit down, the phone started ringing. He would lean forward, snap up the hand piece and shout, "Hel-LO! This is HE! Heyyyyy! How the hell are ya?" and then lean back in his chair, flashing his famous teeth-clenched grin.

Chances were good he was talking to one of his 640 former Michigan players, a dozen of whom called or stopped by every day. Whether they were All-Americans or walk-ons, Schembechler invariably remembered their names, their positions, their hometowns and what they were up to since the last time they talked. Not surprisingly, almost all of them kept in touch. If you played for Bo, you had two fathers.

His voice is still ringing in their ears, long after they've graduated. "Early is on time, and on time is late!" "There is NO substitute for hard work!" and "You know what the right thing to do is—so just do it!"

He wrote their recommendations, attended their weddings and visited their hospital rooms. If he could do anything to help, he would—just like that—including visiting two players in prison, and successfully working to get them back on their feet after they got out.

They all say the same thing: "You may not always have liked it, but with Bo, you always knew exactly where you stood." Bo insulted you to your face and praised you behind your back. In a society that favors image over substance and glad-handing over sincerity, Bo's bedrock values seem almost extreme now.

Schembechler was a man who knew exactly who he was, but seemed mystified by the public's view of him. "Hey, I'm not Jonas Salk," he said. "Football coaching should not have so much status attached to it."

Bo Schembechler converses with a referee in 1969. Image: Robert Kalmbach photograph collection, Bentley Historical Library

Bo Schembechler coaches quarterback Jim Harbaugh in 1984. Image: Robert Kalmbach photograph collection, Bentley Historical Library

Bo didn't get it. His appeal was not based on his victories, but on his values—which were as simple as they were timeless.

When Bo was still coaching, he helped out the Special Olympics by playing basketball with developmentally disabled kids. He loved it because they had no idea who he was, and didn't care. "I was just some old guy who came down to play basketball with them."

That's pretty much how Schembechler saw himself: Just some old guy who once coached football.

We knew better.

THIS IS MICHIGAN

HAIL, HAIL. "The Victors," the University's fight song, was written in 1898 by student Louis Elbel after a rousing U-M football win. Considered by many to be the definitive fight song, "The Victors" was crowned "the best college march ever written" by legendary composer and director John Philip Sousa. The song connects fans with an intercollegiate athletics program that features the nation's largest football stadium, the winged helmet, the winningest football program, hundreds of Olympians and All-Americans, and 56 national championships.

The shades of a Michigan football game. Students adopted "azure blue and maize" as the school colors in 1867. Image: Roger Hart, Michigan Photography

MOMENTS

THE 1913 LECTERN

President Gerald R. Ford uses the 1913 lectern during a Rackham Auditorium ceremony in 2003. Image: Marcia Ledford, Michigan Photography

For more than 100 years, Hill Auditorium has been Michigan's most prestigious venue for rhetoric and debate. And for that same span, speaker after speaker has gripped, pounded, caressed and leaned upon an oak lectern given to the University by students.

Could the Class of 1913 have known the voices of influence, controversy and power that would one day stand at this lectern?

Looking back, it seems only fitting that a piece of furniture that would support some of society's most provocative speakers was itself a point of contention.

When leaders of the 1913 literary class began brainstorming about a class gift, the men suggested something for the Michigan Union. This raised the ire of women, who were not about to contribute money to buy a gift bound for a building reserved for men.

The senior women prevailed, and the class voted to give a reading desk for the University's soon-to-open auditorium. Created by Detroit architect Albert Kahn to complement the great hall he designed, the Hill Auditorium lectern cost $250.

As silent witness to the ideas and arguments that are the stuff of a university, however, the lectern has been priceless.

The Rev. Dr. Martin Luther King Jr. at Hill Auditorium in November 1962. Image: Media Resources Center (University of Michigan) Records, Bentley Historical Library

ROBERT FROST IN ANN ARBOR

"A Joy to Be With"

By James Tobin

On October 10, 1921, the editors of Michigan's student literary magazine, *Whimsies,* each carrying his or her own poems, stepped gingerly into Professor Roy Cowden's house on Olivia Street. Then, one by one, the young writers were introduced to their critic for the evening. He was a New England farmer in his mid-40s—"a not-at-all-trim man of medium stature, in a not-too-well-pressed grey suit, with fair, not-too-tidy hair," recalled one student, Stella Brunt. He was also the most distinguished American poet of his generation, soon to win the first of four Pulitzer Prizes—Robert Frost.

"We had a splendid evening," Stella wrote her mother, "and shall have them hereafter every three weeks. . . . Robert Frost talked to me about fifteen minutes all alone, in a corner. It is genuine joy to be with him: one feels at once hopeless and determined." It was the beginning of a yearlong friendship between Frost and the student writers of Michigan.

The poet was spending the year in Ann Arbor thanks to Marion LeRoy Burton, the charismatic pastor who had just become U-M's sixth president. Burton endorsed the view of Raymond Hughes, president of Miami University of Ohio, who recently had told fellow educators that "nothing would do more to leaven the increasing materialism of the American

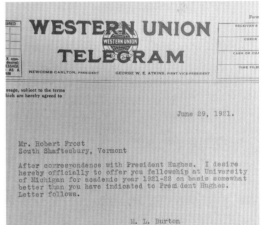

President Marion L. Burton's telegram to poet Robert Frost. Image: Marion L. Burton Papers, Bentley Historical Library

Portrait of Robert Frost by Leon A. Makielski. Image: Robert Frost Collections, Special Collections Library, University of Michigan Library

Robert Frost. Image: Miriam and Ira D. Wallach Division of Art, Prints and Photographs: Photography Collection, The New York Public Library

Robert Frost in the 1922 *Michiganensian*

university than to have a great creative artist working on the campus."

Burton approached Frost with the offer of an eight-month stipend of $5,000 (donated by the U-M regent and former Michigan governor Chase Osborn) to become Michigan's first Fellow in Creative Arts. The poet agreed immediately, telling Burton: "I am somewhat surprised when men of your executive authority . . . see it as a part of their duty to the state to encourage the arts." Frost and Burton had agreed he would teach no regular classes—an arrangement that irritated some off-campus skeptics, including an anonymous writer in the *Washtenaw Post,* who asked if the University ought to pay Frost $5,000 without asking him "to do anything, not even to twirl his thumbs, if he does not so desire."

Frost hoped to write a good deal. But to keep the skeptics at bay, and to justify Burton's trust, he embarked on strenuous rounds of public events and meetings with faculty and students. The editors of *Whimsies* were the prime beneficiaries. At the Cowdens' home, Frost would avoid the big chair set out for him and instead find an "unpretentious, dim corner." According to Frances Swain, another of the *Whimsies,* "he speaks lightly enough," but "there is a lasting significance in [his comments]. The conversation of Frost sparkles . . . and is at its best in the pauses—when it is in his eyes, between words. He is humorous and ruthless. . . . He is so very comfortable that he induces all the *Whimsies* in their private talk of him familiarly to call him plain 'Robert' or 'Frost.'" He was also "an excellent gossip."

His remarks on students' readings were "gentle" but exacting. After one unfortunate performance thudded to a close, he diplomatically broke the silence by saying, "You know, there is a difference between fetching and far-fetching." But even a kindly critique from Robert Frost could wreck a student's spirits, as Stella Brunt could attest after reading four verses aloud one night.

"It was a harrowing experience," she wrote, "especially when Robert Frost kept scolding at me over the same old faults—not making my meaning clear, and using old phrases. My nerves were all on edge to begin with, and that about unsettled me. I didn't sleep all night."

With the *Whimsies,* most of them women, Frost was a gentleman. But one of them, Ruth Lechlitner, glimpsed another side when she and a friend knocked on the door of the Frosts'

ditions of the Fellowship will permit it; we do not know that
Mr. Frost would consider it: we are very certain, each one on
his own behalf, that the Frost stability, the Frost honesty,
the strong, quiet spirit of the man, is leaving its mark upon
the student body, and that this is exactly the kind of a mark
that Michigan wants to see upon all of her sons and her daugh-
ters.   We are sure that you will give due consideration to our
request.

                Very respectfully yours,
            The Friends and Supporters of Whimsies

Frost was so popular that students lobbied President Burton to keep him at Michigan. Image: Marion L. Burton Papers, Bentley Historical Library

rented house at 1523 Washtenaw.

"Robert, in a well-worn grey sweater, opened it to us," Lechlitner recalled long afterward. "He greeted me cordially, but his interest was obviously in Dee, an unusually pretty girl, and one of the first to have her hair cut in a short, curled 'bob.' Moreover, she had fastened her knickers well above the knee, displaying a pair of very shapely legs. I saw Frost's swift downward glance, and an elfish glint in his eye. At this, I think I liked him better than I had at any time before."

The poet was such a hit that President Burton said he didn't know who was more admired—Fielding Yost or Robert Frost. With realistic humility, Frost said he would schedule the next poetry reading during a Michigan football game and see which drew the larger crowd.

Frost bent to pressure to return for another year, though

bad health made that stay less successful. (He wrote his most famous work, "Stopping by Woods on a Snowy Evening," during the summer between his first and second Ann Arbor sojourns.) Burton brought Frost back for a third fellowship in 1925–26 and sealed an arrangement to make the appointment permanent. But when Burton died soon after of a heart attack, Frost decided his ties to New England were stronger than his commitment to U-M, and he changed his mind—though "I like Michigan people and I like Michigan."

Robert Frost in Ann Arbor. Image: Robert Frost Collections, Special Collections Library, University of Michigan Library

THIS IS MICHIGAN

THE WRITTEN WORD. Michigan's rich literary tradition includes playwright Arthur Miller, poet Joseph Brodsky, Caldecott Medal winner Chris Van Allsburg, and the prestigious Hopwood Awards, a contest program for students that has launched dozens of notable writers stretching from novelists Betty Smith ("A Tree Grows in Brooklyn") and Elizabeth Kostova ("The Historian") to poets Jane Kenyon, Donald Hall and Robert Hayden. Other Hopwood winners include National Book Award winner Jesmyn Ward ("Salvage the Bones") and Chigozie Obioma, whose debut novel "The Fishermen" was longlisted for the Man Booker Prize.

Arthur Miller during a 1973 visit to campus. Image: Bob Kalmbach, Michigan Photography

DRAKE'S

Limeade for Generations

By James Tobin

When Herbert Hoover was president of the United States, a young fellow named Truman Tibbals took a job washing dishes for 35 cents an hour at Drake's Sandwich Shop, 709 N. University. He worked his way up to waiting tables, and after a while he bought the place from old Mr. Drake.

He made just one change. He took out the tables and installed high-walled booths. From that day until he sold the shop when Bill Clinton was president, Truman Tibbals left everything else pretty much the same, including the name over the candy-stripe awning in front. Through the Great Depression, World War II, the Baby Boom, the Beatles, Vietnam, Watergate, disco, and President Ronald Reagan, Drake's sold chocolate cordials, orange marmalade sandwiches, pecan rolls, and limeade (fresh-squeezed, with the rind in the glass) to three generations of University of Michigan students. They adored the place.

The walls were a milky, Depression-era green, like faded linoleum. Shelves held scores of glass jars filled with tea (Alfalfa Mint, Travencore, and Constant Comment among them) and even more of candy—jelly beans, candy corn, rum raisins, malted milk balls, cherry cordials, strawberry cordials, raspberry cordials, shelf above shelf. Candy went out the door in bags adorned in red and white stripes, like the awning outside.

The sandwich menu included the "American

Drake's Sandwich Shop in the 1930s. Image: Sam Sturgis Collection, Bentley Historical Library

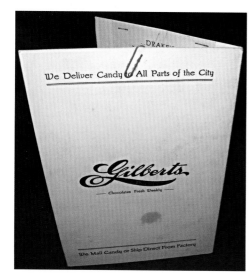

Drake's Sandwich Shop, menu, with LOW prices. Images: Courtesy Wystan Stevens, Creative Commons CC By 2.0

cheese," the "bacon and peanut butter," the "chopped green olive nut," the "cucumber and tomato," and the "head lettuce" sandwich. Ten specialty sandwiches (double-deckers on toast) included the "Harvard" (boiled ham, lettuce, tomato, and mayonnaise), the "Princeton" (American cheese, lettuce, tomato, and mayonnaise), and the "Michigan" (chicken, lettuce, tomato, and mayonnaise). You wrote your own order with a tiny pencil on a green soda-shop pad.

The staff comprised Mr. Tibbals, Mrs. Tibbals, and a team of waitresses (plus the occasional waiter), many of whom appeared to be trained in the owners' distinctly taciturn style of service. For people who dispensed small pleasures for a living, the Tibbalses made a gloomy pair. They often could be seen perched on counter stools, well apart from each other, glowering at the wait staff. Students found them fearsome. But Mr. Tibbals was a pal of the Ann Arbor police, who often rolled in for breaks late at night.

The Tibbalses did bring in the occasional new item. They served toasted bagels with cream cheese years before bagel franchises spread through the Midwest, and they were early providers of Gummi bears. In the '40s Mr. Tibbals opened the room upstairs for records and dancing. First it was the Walnut Room, later the Martian Room, but in the shop's last decades the stairs were closed and the only thing left of the Martian Room was the sign. For a time there was dancing downstairs, too, and a burger bar in the back. But the innovations always faded, and back the Tibbalses would go to the candy, the tea, the limeade, and the sandwiches.

When the *Michigan Alumnus* solicited memories of Drake's from readers, a surprising number said they had dated their future spouses there. The privacy of the tall-walled booths fostered intimacy. The "Coke date," a perennial getting-to-know-you ritual, was popular at Drake's, which was located just steps from the Michigan and State theaters. One night in January 1969, Rick and Roberta London got engaged at the corner of South University and Washtenaw, then strolled across the Diag to mark the occasion at Drake's.

"I will forever associate the small wooden benches, a toasted bagel, and cup of tea at Drake's with the wonderful emotions of that day," Roberta London remembered.

Another who wrote in was Ron Marabate, who—also in the late 1960s—would soothe his mind with a cinnamon roll on North U after rigorous German classes in the Frieze Building. "Drake's was also memorable whenever I was joined there by a young lady," he wrote, "especially the one who later became my wife. I don't remember much of my Deutsch, but Drake's is still vivid in my mind." Mr. Tibbals died in 1993. The place was sold about the same time.

DEWEY, TRUMAN AND ISR'S POLLSTERS

By Susan Rosegrant

The two questions were tacked on at the last minute to a survey on foreign policy from the University of Michigan:

"In the presidential elections next month, are you almost certain to vote, uncertain, or won't you vote?"

(If certain or uncertain) "Do you plan to vote Republican, Democratic, or something else?"

The questions weren't even the point of the survey. But the answers and their impact helped to launch a far-ranging new field of study at the fledgling Institute for Social Research (ISR) and to establish electoral behavior as a discipline in political science. They also shone a light on polling and sampling methodology nationwide.

Making Headlines

It was the fall of 1948, and incumbent President Harry S. Truman was embroiled in a grueling campaign against Republican challenger Thomas E. Dewey. Truman's popularity was low, even among Democrats. As the election neared, the national press corps—relying largely on the reports of the three major pollsters, Gallup, Roper and Crossley—was bluntly predicting an easy Dewey victory.

That's when U-M's Survey Research Center (SRC) unwittingly stepped in. Researcher Robert Kahn was working with ISR founder Angus Campbell on a study of public attitudes toward foreign policy for the State Department. As an afterthought, they threw in two questions to gauge the political interests and orientations of the respondents.

After leaving the White House, President Harry Truman re-created the photo of him holding the famous *Chicago Daily Tribune* issue of 1948. Image: Copyright unknown, Courtesy of Harry S. Truman Library

Kahn and Campbell ran their survey in October, finishing shortly before the Nov. 2 election. The sample of 610 prospective voters was too small to make any predictions about the forthcoming election, and that wasn't what their research was about anyway. Still, as the survey responses came in and Kahn posted them on a blackboard, a surprising trend began to emerge: The two candidates were running neck and neck, with Truman slightly ahead, and more than 20 percent of voters still undecided.

Kahn and his wife, Bea, hunkered down by their home radio on election night to listen to the results come in. By late in the evening, broadcasters began questioning the predicted Dewey triumph; by morning, they were announcing one of the greatest upsets in American election history. As Truman, the newly re-elected president, headed from his home in Missouri back to Washington, D.C., the train paused in St. Louis and a photographer snapped the now-famous photo of Truman grinning and holding a copy of the *Chicago Tribune* declaring Dewey the winner.

Red-faced Pollsters

The very public failure of the predictions shook commercial polling operations to their core. In fact, the negative fallout was so widespread that SRC director Rensis Likert felt compelled to declare in a *Scientific American* article that "it would be as foolish to abandon this field as it would be to give up any scientific inquiry which, because of faulty methods and analysis, produced inaccurate results."

SRC certainly had no intentions of abandoning the field. Immediately after the election, Kahn and Campbell decided to go back to the respondents from the first survey. This time, their questions would be firmly focused on how voters had behaved in the just-completed election.

With new data in hand, Kahn and Campbell began to draw conclusions. Pollsters had drastically underrated the importance of undecided voters, apparently assuming they would either not vote or would split along the lines of committed voters. But in fact, late deciders went 2–1 for Truman.

Pollsters also misunderstood how much could change in the final weeks or even days of the campaign: Roper stopped polling in September, and Gallup and Crossley in early October. But one-eighth of those who claimed to have voted said they didn't choose a candidate until the last two weeks before Election Day.

Lastly, pollsters appeared to accept that respondents would do what they said they planned to do, but that often wasn't the case. Some who said they would vote didn't; some who said they wouldn't, did. Moreover, a significant number of "committed" voters changed their minds, with more changing from Dewey to Truman.

ISR Director Angus Campbell, right, with Philip Converse and Warren E. Miller of the Survey Research Center's National Elections Study. Image: University of Michigan News and Information Service, Bentley Historical Library

A Turning Point

SRC wasn't the only organization evaluating what had happened. The Social Science Research Council convened a group to evaluate what had gone wrong; a few months later, the Committee on Analysis of Pre-Election Polls and Forecasts delivered a verdict that largely agreed with SRC's conclusions.

The committee suggested that pollsters had relied on unscientific methods. At the time, commercial polling firms like Gallup and Roper all did quota sampling. Interviewers sought out certain quotas of respondents—such as male or female, young or old—within set geographical areas. But because how they selected those respondents was largely up to them, interviewers might, for example, go mainly to affluent neighborhoods, excluding poor and middle-class residents and biasing the results.

By contrast, SRC used a more time-consuming and costly approach known as probability or random geographic sampling. For the foreign policy survey, they chose clusters of counties across the country, and then randomly sampled the populations in those areas, giving every resident of voting age an equal chance of being chosen. SRC didn't invent these techniques—they were developed in the 1930s. But SRC was refining them and putting them to new uses.

The hard look at sampling that resulted from Truman's unexpected win was a turning point in survey methodology. Writing in 1998, Humphrey Taylor, head of the Louis Harris polling firm, declared, "Virtually all public opinion surveys conducted in the United States since then—whether conducted face-to-face or by telephone—have used some modified version of probability (or random) sampling. Indeed, for American researchers quota sampling is almost a dirty phrase."

THIS IS MICHIGAN

COMPUTER WIZARDS. From alumnus Claude Shannon, the father of information theory, and Irma Wyman, the first woman to be chief information officer at Honeywell, to the creation and impact of Google, U-M and its graduates have forever altered the sharing of knowledge through technology. Shannon's work in the 1930s was essential to U-M establishing one of the world's first computer science programs in 1956. Michigan engineers in 1988 built a computing backbone to connect and support thousands of researchers across the country—an achievement essential to the birth of the Internet. U-M was the first public university to partner with Google to digitize the University Library's nearly seven million volumes, revolutionizing the sharing of knowledge. Google itself is the brainchild of engineering alumnus Larry Page, who co-created the search engine with Sergey Brin.

Google co-founder and U-M alumnus Larry Page speaks at 2009 commencement. Image: Scott C. Soderberg, Michigan Photography

JFK AT THE UNION
"There is a Greater Purpose"

By James Tobin

Senator John F. Kennedy's motorcade rolled into Ann Arbor very early on the morning of Friday, Oct. 14, 1960. The election was three and a half weeks away. The Democratic nominee for president and his staff had just flown into Willow Run Airport. A few hours earlier, in New York, Kennedy had challenged Vice President Richard Nixon, the Republican nominee, in the third of their four nationally televised debates. The race was extremely close, and Michigan was up for grabs. Kennedy's schedule called for a few hours of sleep, then a one-day whistle-stop train tour across the state.

Welcoming Committee

The campaign got word that students had been waiting outside the Michigan Union, where Kennedy was to spend the night, for three hours. As the cars reached the corner of State and South University, Kennedy's speechwriters, Theodore Sorensen and Richard Goodwin, looked out the window. Students, densely packed, were milling all over the steps and sidewalks and into the street. Cries arose as the cars pulled up.

"He won't just let them stand there," Sorensen told Goodwin. "He's going to speak. Maybe that'll give us a chance to get something to eat."

They hadn't prepared a speech, but Kennedy was good at extemporizing in a pinch. He might

Candidate John F. Kennedy on the Michigan Union steps in the early hours of Oct. 14, 1960. Image: Eck Stanger, News and Information Services Collection, Bentley Historical Library

have given the students a quick greeting and a standard pitch for votes. No one knows why he chose, instead, to ask a question that would launch the signature program of his administration and ignite the idealism of a generation.

A Platform of Peace

Since early in the campaign year, there had been scattered proposals for a volunteer corps of young Americans who would go abroad to help nations emerging from colonialism in Africa and Asia. Kennedy had asked for studies of the idea, including from Samuel Hayes, a U-M professor of economics and director of the Center for Research on Economic Development. In early October, his staff had floated the idea in a press release, but no sparks had been struck. And Kennedy, according to aides, had been leery of the idea, fearing the damage Nixon might cause, in the jittery atmosphere of the Cold War, by calling him naïve about foreign affairs.

Possibly it was a remark of Nixon's that drew Kennedy's mind back to the idea. In the debate the night before, the vice president had reminded the national audience that three Democratic presidents—Woodrow Wilson, Franklin Roosevelt and Harry Truman—had taken the nation to war. Kennedy may have wanted to strike a note that would associate his campaign with peace.

In any case, he did not actually propose a program. He issued a challenge.

Speaking into a microphone at the center of the stone staircase, Kennedy began by expressing his "thanks to you, as a graduate of the Michigan of the East, Harvard University." The campaign, he said, was the most important since the Depression election of 1932, "because of the problems which press upon the United States, and the opportunities which will be presented to us in the 1960s, which must be seized."

Then he asked his question:

"How many of you who are going to be doctors are willing to spend your days in Ghana? Technicians or engineers: how many of you are willing to work in the Foreign Service and spend your lives traveling around the world? On your willingness to do that, not merely to serve one year or two years in the service, but on your willingness to contribute part of your life to this country, I think will depend the answer whether a free society can compete. I think it can. And I think

Americans are willing to contribute. But the effort must be far greater than we've ever made in the past.

"Therefore, I am delighted to come to Michigan, this university, because unless we have those resources in this school, unless you comprehend the nature of what is being asked of you, this country can't possibly move through the next 10 years in a period of relative strength."

A Winning Number

He said he'd come to Ann Arbor merely "to go to bed"— drawing a ribald roar from the crowd—then: "This is the longest short speech I've ever made, and I'll therefore finish it." The state had not built the university "merely to help its graduates have an economic advantage in the life struggle," he said. "There is certainly a greater purpose, and I'm sure you recognize it." He was not merely asking for their votes, but for "your support for this country over the next decade."

The students roared again. Then Kennedy went up to bed.

That was it. He had spoken for three minutes. There were 50 or 60 reporters with Kennedy, but few mentioned the senator's remarks. Russell Baker of the *New York Times* reported that during JFK's entire swing through Michigan, he said "nothing that was new"—which was true, if one counted the early-October press release. But in the aftermath of the speech, something new began.

The following Tuesday, Oct. 18, U.S. Rep. Chester Bowles of Connecticut, a Kennedy supporter and adviser, spoke to students in the Michigan Union ballroom. He, too, proposed what the *Daily* called "a U.N. civil service, which would send doctors, agricultural experts, and teachers to needy countries throughout the world."

Among Bowles' listeners were two married graduate students, Alan and Judy Guskin. From Bowles' talk, they went to a diner where they drafted a letter to the *Daily* on a napkin. The letter was published the following Friday. The Guskins noted that Kennedy and Bowles had "emphasized that disarmament and peace lie to a very great extent in our hands and requested our participation throughout the world as necessary for the realization of these goals." The two then pledged to "devote a number of years to work in countries where our help is needed," and they challenged other students to write similar pledges to Kennedy and Bowles.

A marker commemorates JFK's speech at the Michigan Union. Image: Scott C. Soderberg, Michigan Photography

The Birth of a Movement

Over the next two weeks, events moved fast. Samuel Hayes, the professor who had written the position paper on a youth corps for Kennedy, contacted the Guskins. Together, they called a mass meeting. Some 250 students came out to sign a petition saying they would volunteer. Hundreds more signers followed within days.

Then Mildred Jeffrey, a Democratic state committeewoman and UAW official whose daughter attended U-M, got word to Ted Sorensen about what Kennedy and Bowles had wrought in Ann Arbor. Sorensen told Kennedy.

On Nov. 2, in a major address in San Francisco, Kennedy formally proposed "a peace corps of talented young men and women, willing and able to serve their country . . . for three years as an alternative or as a supplement to peacetime selective service." (Nixon responded by calling the idea "a cult of escapism" and "a haven for draft dodgers.")

On Sunday, Nov. 6, two days before the election, Kennedy was expected at the Toledo airport. Three carloads of U-M students, including the Guskins, drove down to show him the petitions. "He took them in his hands and started looking through the names," Judy Guskin recalled later. "He was very interested."

Alan asked: "Are you really serious about the Peace Corps?"

"Until Tuesday we'll worry about this nation," Kennedy said. "After Tuesday, the world."

Two days later, Kennedy defeated Nixon by some 120,000 votes, one of the slimmest margins in U.S. history. Some argue the Peace Corps proposal may have swayed enough votes to make the difference.

"It might still be just an idea but for the affirmative response of those Michigan students and faculty," wrote Sargent Shriver, JFK's brother-in-law and the Peace Corps' first director, in his memoir. "Possibly Kennedy would have tried it once more on some other occasion, but without a strong popular response he would have concluded the idea was impractical or premature. That probably would have ended it then and there. Instead, it was almost a case of spontaneous combustion."

Alan and Judy Guskin were among the Peace Corps' early volunteers. They served in Thailand.

THIS IS MICHIGAN

INTERNATIONAL REACH. U-M can trace its global reach to the late 1840s and neighboring Canada, home of the first international student, and China, where Judson Collins—a member of the first graduating class—served as a Methodist missionary. It launched a legacy of global connections. President James B. Angell served the U.S. government as Minister to China in 1880–81. The first student from Asia (Japan) enrolled in 1872, the first from Puerto Rico in 1877, and the first from Africa (Natal, today's South Africa) in 1884. The Barbour Scholarships have supported women students from Asian countries for 100 years. Today, U-M routinely leads the country's public universities in students receiving Fulbright grants to study internationally.

Studying abroad in Marrakech, Morocco, in 2009. Image: Christine Brash, U-M International Institute

EARTH DAY EVE

By James Tobin

In the fall of 1969, after long hours in the lab, U-M grad students in zoology and botany often wound up at the big round tables at Metzger's on Washington Street. Over pitchers of beer, discussion often turned to the seabirds killed in that year's oil spill off Santa Barbara, California; to the Cuyahoga River in Cleveland, so clogged with oil that the river itself had caught fire; and to the mats of algae so dense on the surface of Lake Erie that rats could be seen scuttling across the lake. Then one night the topic shifted from pollution to what should be done about it. The students learned that friends in the School of Natural Resources were thinking the same way, and the casual bull sessions turned into serious meetings.

Some of them had been in Ann Arbor in 1965, when U-M students held the first teach-in on the war in Vietnam. The same approach could work now, they thought, but it should be even bigger.

"Working Through the System"

"It was decided early that if we were going to do something, it had to be different from most university activism events, which just involved university personnel," recalled John Russell, who had just left the botany program to teach biology and conservation at Ann Arbor Pioneer High School. "And it had to include all aspects of the community, all political parties, all ethnic groups. So it was to be a very comprehensive thing. It was the end of the '60s. There was nothing wrong with dreaming big."

A Crisler Arena crowd waits for the kick-off rally on the Teach-In's first evening. Image: News and Information Services Collection, Bentley Historical Library

133

They started a group called Environmental Action for Survival, or ENACT. Members of the steering committee ranged from quiet lab types to veteran protesters such as Stephen Sporn, a member of Students for a Democratic Society. Yet overall it was "a very conservative movement," Russell recalled. "We put less emphasis on protest activism and much more on education and policy. We did not want to be seen as radical extremists, but rather as mainstream agents of change who were working through the 'system.' This point has been dramatically overlooked in many accounts. We discussed and scrapped plans for protests and banner-waving and sit-ins."

Declaring "Our sick environment needs you!" they called a mass meeting of interested students and announced plans for a massive, multi-day teach-in the following spring. And, right away, ENACT's leaders began talking with staff in the office of U.S. Sen. Gaylord Nelson, D-Wis.

Nelson had come to national prominence in the late 1950s as Wisconsin's "Conservation Governor." Elected to the Senate in 1962, he had spent the '60s urging attention to the degradation of the American landscape—pollution, sprawl, littering, the loss of wilderness—but with little success. Now, the mounting squalor of water and air pollution was finally attracting press coverage and enflaming public worries. Nelson sensed a propitious moment. Just after touring the site of the Santa Barbara oil spill, he read an article on teach-ins as levers for political action. Within days, he was floating the idea of a nationwide teach-in on what people were calling "the environmental crisis"—at just the time ENACT was organizing in Ann Arbor.

Fighting the Calendar

Gaylord Nelson had a big idea, but he didn't know much about teach-ins. So in November 1969, he brought in Doug Scott, a U-M student in natural resources and co-chair of ENACT, to help plan the national event, to be called Earth Day.

Scott brought to Washington a memo spelling out the steps ENACT had been taking to organize its own event. Nelson's staff made copies and sent them out to anyone who asked how they, too, could take part in Earth Day.

Meanwhile, in Ann Arbor, the academic calendar was giving ENACT a problem. Senator Nelson had set the date of

Earth Day as April 22, 1970, so that it would fall before final exam periods at most U.S. colleges and universities. But not at the University of Michigan, where, by the trimester system, April 22 would come smack in the middle of exams. ENACT had no choice but to schedule its event earlier. The organizers chose March 11–14. The event was formally titled, simply, the "Teach-In on the Environment."

That winter there were scattered pro-environment events on several campuses, including a one-day rally at Northwestern. But none matched ENACT's ambition and scope.

The organizers planned four days of events across Ann Arbor. They booked Crisler Arena for the opening night. They packed the speakers' schedule with major names—Maine Sen. Edmund Muskie, the front-runner for the 1972 Democratic

Students gather on the Diag during Michigan's 1970 Teach-In on the Environment. Image: News and Information Services Collection, Bentley Historical Library

An iconic poster of a pensive boy with an overcrowded planet Earth became well known during the four days of the Teach-In. Image: Courtesy of John Russell

presidential nomination; social critic Ralph Nader; and Dr. Barry Commoner, an eloquent biologist who had become a guru to the emerging movement. They invited Hollywood celebrities who were worried about pollution—not young firebrands like Jane Fonda but old-timers like Arthur Godfrey and Eddie Albert—and industrialists who wanted to tell their side of the story. They got commitments from entertainers including Gordon Lightfoot, Odetta, and the Chicago cast of *Hair*.

Most programs were to be genuinely educational, including workshops for some 20,000 schoolchildren. No one knew if the public would respond.

"A Big Deal"

By the time the program started, organizers were scrambling to set up loudspeakers in the Crisler parking lot. Three thousand people had to stand outside. Over four days, an estimated 50,000 people took part in ENACT's teach-in—an astonishing success that fueled enthusiasm for Senator Nelson's national Earth Day, which drew some 20 million participants four weeks later and transformed environmentalism into a movement of historic importance.

"The Michigan event was by far the biggest, best, and most influential of the pre-Earth Day teach-ins," Adam Rome, a historian and authority on the environmental movement, told the *Ann Arbor Chronicle*. "It was the first sign that Earth Day would be a big deal."

THIS IS MICHIGAN

CAMPUS ACTIVISM. Social activism at Michigan shaped several critical movements of the 1960s that continue to resonate in the 21st century: the Peace Corps, the Vietnam teach-in, civil rights and Earth Day. U-M's penchant for activism also was responsible for two nationwide yet divergent movements: the 1892 formation of College Republicans, which remains the voice of young conservatives in the 21st century, and the 1960 establishment of Students for a Democratic Society, whose manifesto, "The Port Huron Statement," launched the New Left.

President Lyndon B. Johnson used Michigan Stadium to unveil his "Great Society" program in 1964. Image: News and Information Services Collection, Bentley Historical Library

ALEXA I. CANADY
B.S., M.D.
Lansing, Michigan
University of Michigan
CAA
Galens
BMA
Patient Care Committee
Victor Vaughan Society
Neurosurgery

MADONNA SLEPT HERE

By Kaitlyn DelBene

When Michigan students move into residence halls and apartment buildings, they occupy the homes of former students who have gone on to change the world with their words, ideas and actions.

There is no guarantee that fame comes with living in a space once occupied by Madonna, who attended from 1976–78 (University Towers, Apt. 10A), 1986 alumnus Jim Harbaugh (South Quad, 6613 Gomberg) or Lucy Liu, who graduated in 1990 (South Quad, 4809 Taylor). But it does make for a distinctive inheritance that shows anything is possible after leaving Ann Arbor.

Authors and Journalists

Judith Guest (Education, 1958)
   Author of bestselling novel *Ordinary People.*
   Lived: 3004 Stockwell
Lawrence Kasdan (LSA, 1970; Education, 1972)
   Producer, director and writer of *The Big Chill, Star Wars* and *Raiders of the Lost Ark.*
   Lived: East Quad, 427 Tyler
Susan Orlean (LSA, 1977)
   Author of *The Orchid Thief,* made into the film *Adaptation.*
   Lived: Alice Lloyd, 6070 Hinsdale
William Shawn (attended 1925–27)
   Longtime editor of the *New Yorker.*
   Lived: 408 Thompson St.

Photos (*left to right, top to bottom*): Mike Wallace, Ann B. Davis, Barry Larkin, Tom Harmon, James Earl Jones (Bentley Historical Library); Darren Criss (University Productions); Alexa Canady (Michiganensian); Jessy Norman (University Productions)

Mike Wallace (LSA, 1939)
>Investigative journalist and original correspondent for CBS' *60 Minutes*.
>Lived: 536 Thompson St.

Athletes

Janet Guthrie (LSA, 1960)
>First woman to compete in the Indianapolis 500 and Daytona 500.
>Lived: East Quad, 207 Prescott

Tom Harmon (LSA, 1941)
>First Wolverine to win the Heisman Trophy.
>Lived: 602 Monroe

Derek Jeter (attended 1992)
>Left in his freshman year for the New York Yankees.
>Lived: 5506 Couzens

Barry Larkin (LSA, 1986)
>Hall-of-Fame shortstop for the Cincinnati Reds.
>Lived: West Quad, 24 Wenley

Engineers, Doctors and Scientists

Alexa Canady (LSA, 1971; Medicine, 1975)
>First African-American woman neurosurgeon.
>Lived: Alice Lloyd, 5508 Palmer

Tony Fadell (Engineering, 1991)
>Inventor of the iPod.
>Lived: East Quad, 222 Hayden

Sanjay Gupta (LSA, 1990; Medicine, 1993)
>Neurosurgeon and CNN chief medical correspondent.
>Lived: East Quad, 330 Hayden

Larry Page (Engineering, 1994)
>Co-founder of Google.
>Lived: 2108 Couzens

Performing Artists

Darren Criss (Music, Theatre & Dance, 2009)
    Actor known for TV series *Glee*.
    Lived: Baits, 1204 Coman

Ann B. Davis (Music, Theatre & Dance, 1948)
    Actress best known as Alice in *The Brady Bunch*.
    Lived: 3523 Stockwell

James Earl Jones (LSA, 1955)
    Winner of Emmy, Tony and Golden Globe awards.
    Lived: West Quad, 214 Allen Rumsey

Jessye Norman (Music, 1968)
    World-renowned opera singer.
    Lived: Baits I, 2002 Smith

Gilda Radner (attended 1964–67)
    Original cast member of *Saturday Night Live*.
    Lived: Alice Lloyd, 6503 Palmer

Gilda Radner. Image: Ann Arbor Civic Theatre

A THIRD CENTURY OF MICHIGAN AMBITION

This young University, shall we not carry it forward to perfection? Is not the ambition worthy of a free and independent people which would make it one of the great Universities of the world, where all knowledges are to be found, where great and good men are to be reared up, and whence shall go forth the light and law of universal education?

—HENRY PHILIP TAPPAN

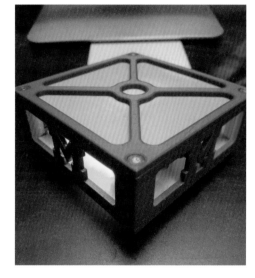

A prototype of the bicentennial time capsule, measuring approximately 3 x 10 x 10 cm and designed for launch into space. Image courtesy Michigan Bicentennial Archive

As the University of Michigan enters its third century, students are developing a time capsule for launch into space. The Michigan Bicentennial Archive would orbit Earth carrying a DNA radiation experiment, encrypted interviews with 1,000 members of the U-M community, and a tiny, physical piece of the Ann Arbor campus. Its orbit is intended to last a century.

President Henry P. Tappan's desire to see an observatory rise from a raw 19th century campus established Michigan as a leader in scientific study and advanced research. Michigan students and alumni have explored the oceans and the solar system. They have floated in space and walked on the moon. As the M-BARC capsule is prepared for launch in the 21st century, its creators and payload embody the realities of Tappan's vision.

What has yet to be produced is the knowledge needed to retrieve the time capsule and return it for Michigan's tricentennial. That will be among the pursuits of the University of Michigan in the next 100 years.

AUTHORS

John U. Bacon is a best-selling author whose books include *Bo's Lasting Lessons: The Legendary Coach Teaches the Timeless Fundamentals of Leadership* and *Endzone: The Rise, Fall, and Return of Michigan Football.*

Francis X. Blouin Jr., Ph.D., professor of history and professor in the School of Information, is chair of the University of Michigan Bicentennial Advisory Committee. He was the director of the Bentley Historical Library from 1981 to 2013.

Kim Clarke is director of communications for the University of Michigan bicentennial. A writer and editor, she manages the U-M Heritage Project.

Kaitlyn DelBene is a 2016 graduate of the University of Michigan Law School. As an undergraduate, she was a researcher and writer for the U-M Heritage Project.

Whitley Hill is a writer and musician whose albums include *We Are Here* and *Farsighted.*

Terrence J. McDonald, Ph.D., is the director of the Bentley Historical Library, Arthur F. Thurnau Professor, and Professor of History.

Susan Rosegrant teaches narrative journalism, non-fiction writing, and creative writing at the U-M Residential College. She is co-author of *Breakthrough International Negotiation: How Great Negotiators Transformed the World's Toughest Post-Cold War Conflicts* and *Route 128: Lessons from Boston's High-Tech Community.*

James Tobin, Ph.D., is an award-winning author, historian and educator. He is professor of journalism at Miami University (Ohio), where he teaches literary journalism. His books include *Ernie Pyle's War: America's Eyewitness to World War II* and *The Man He Became: How FDR Defied Polio to Win the Presidency.*

STORY CREDITS

Reprinted by permission of *Michigan Today:*
   "Remembering Bo" (November 2006)
   "JFK at the Union" (January 3, 2008)
   "Earth Day Eve" (March 10, 2010)
   "Robert Frost in Ann Arbor" (June 9, 2010)
   "One Odd Duck" (May 11, 2011)
   "Limeade and Love: Memories of Drake's Sandwich
   Shop" (June 20, 2012)
   "Who Was James Angell?" (July 29, 2013)
Reprinted by permission of *U-M Heritage Project:*
   "Dear Aunt Ruth" (February 2013)
   "The 1913 Lectern" (February 2013)
   "Revelli: The Long Note" (February 2013)
   "A Creation of My Own" (February 2013)
   "Wallenberg at Michigan" (February 2013)
   "Madonna Slept Here" (July 2013)
   "Professor White's Diag" (October 2014)
   "Doc Losh" (May 2015)
   "First in Class" (January 2016)
Reprinted by permission of *ISR Sampler:*
   "ISR and the Truman/Dewey Upset" (Spring 2012)
Reprinted by permission of Bentley Historical Library
Collections:
   "The Mystery Above the Pillars" (Spring 2015)
Reprinted by permission of *Medicine at Michigan:*
   "Quiet Pioneer" (Spring–Summer 2008)
Reprinted by permission of author, Francis X. Blouin:
   "The Origins of a Reputation: The University of
   Michigan and the Angell Years"